"As a teenager, it seems there are always new things to deal with that feel like the end of the world. *On the PATH* has taught me that the tools and mindset of someone on the PATH can make a world of difference. With them in hand, those problems become manageable and not so scary."

Amanda, 15

"I am the farthest thing from perfect. However, that's okay because I know now that I'm *On the PATH,* and I can work on being a better me today and every day for the rest of my existence."

Kendall, 18

"As a teenager, I tend to use my 'blame thrower' quite often, whether dealing with an unacceptable grade or an event that has consequences I don't want to face. *On the PATH* has helped me analyze my thinking and identify where the responsibility truly lies: square on my shoulders. My trust in the never-ending love of Jesus allows me to look inward and see the truth."

Taylor, 18

"I'm a big fan of *On the PATH.* The material is engaging and interactive, and students who use it will find their religion classes useful, relevant, and definitely interesting. I found myself always learning something important, and wanting to learn more."

Matt, 17

"The concepts and lingo in *On the PATH* are so much more where teens are as compared to what is usually offered in religion programs. The examples it offers are concrete, germane, and easy for them to relate to. Students will find themselves engaged, investigating, and taking responsibility for their own faith and moral development."

Jan, teacher

"Let *On the PATH* take your faith to the next level by teaching you how to let God into your life through small, but powerful, actions."

Lindsey, 15

"*On the PATH* gives students tools to face daily challenges and provides strategies for putting on the armor of God and taking control of their lives. They learn it is a choice to take action and stop being a victim. The lessons in these pages are useful, empowering, relevant, and faith-filled."

Christine, teacher

"Before reading this book I had a whole different mindset about how to live my life. *On the PATH* has helped me realize what truly matters: it's all about learning from your choices, how you react to them, and letting your faith be a central part of the experience."

Anna, 16

First printing

ISBN: 978-0-692-36466-6
On the Path Books
13 Forest Knoll Circle
Lake Saint Louis, Missouri
Phone: 314-503-3053
Email: peg@onthepathbooks.com
www.onthepathbooks.com

Following Jesus

On the PATH

A Catholic Teen's Guide to Life-Altering Faith

Peg Dubrowski

Illustrations by Tim Parlin

Table of Contents

Foreward

Peg Dubrowski has been formed by the power of faith. She has come to live in the presence of God as a compassionate and patient Father and Jesus as a faithful and loving brother whose Spirit is ever present in her life. Living in God's grace, she is filled with the wonder of God's creation, with gratitude for daily blessings, and with understanding for the purpose of God's beloved sons and daughters.

Peg has also listened deeply to the inner lives of young people. With the Spirit of God's compassion and understanding, Peg speaks a language of wisdom to them that can be trusted and embraced in their own lives. This book encourages and provides youth with a path for pursuing the challenge of becoming their true selves.

Reading *On the PATH* as a life-long Catholic, my own faith has been strengthened, my sins more humbly acknowledged and my purpose more clearly understood. Yes, Peg has written this book for youth, but it is a gospel, a message of good news, for anyone seeking to live in the light and enjoy the peace and fullness of life that comes from living more deeply in union with God and the human family.

As Director of Top 20 Training, I am grateful to Peg for weaving several Top 20 concepts and principles into the journey of young people as they seek to develop the best version of themselves and a deeper relationship with friends, family and God.

Students and adults reading *On the PATH* will be left with a greater sense of hope as they become more aware of the God-given power within themselves to make a positive difference in the quality of their lives, relationships and experiences. Peg's book provides a meaningful connection to God that all young people need if they are to maintain their wholeness and holiness as they meet the challenges of living in a 21st century world.

Paul Bernabei
Director
Top 20 Training

Introduction

A guidebook to life-altering faith?

Really?

Yep. That's what the cover says.

Discovering life-altering faith is like code-breaking. You begin with a bunch of gibberish (for instance, all that stuff you've been learning in religion class or PSR). The gibberish promises to be hugely meaningful but you have to figure out how all the pieces fit together. Once you find a single key you can begin decoding the gibberish and find its true meaning and value.

I've taught Catholic teenagers for a long, long time. While all my lesson plans were highly entertaining and super motivating (of course), shortly into the whole teaching thing I realized that no matter what I taught, you were always more interested in the really important stuff. You leaned in and found your voice when our class time meandered to places more pressing to you: getting caught up in gossip, subjects that seem pointless and teachers who bore you, convincing your parents that, "Yes, I love you, but I want to go to the mall anyway," why so-and-so is good at everything while you are average at most things, the nasty language used in the locker room, and the nonstop text-bullying that led to a teenager's suicide. You may have thought you were thwarting my lesson plan, but you were actually trying to break the code. **You have been searching for life-altering faith.**

Consider the book in your hands as a manual for code-breaking. Rather than pump you with gibberish about faith, it's going to help you decode the puzzle by living it rather than learning it. Why this approach? Because the key to life-altering faith is its ability to answer the pressing and constant questions of life, such as:

- How can I stay out of their fight?
- Why shouldn't I if everyone else is?
- Who can I depend on?
- What am I supposed to be getting out of this anyway?
- What will happen if I stand up to them?
- Isn't there more to life than this?

You have my promise that the pages ahead will not feel 'textbooky.' Faith is tremendously personal, so I've written in the first person and speak directly to you, and I've used a bunch of examples from my own life (permission granted from my kids as needed) so you'll get to know me. Occasional Faith Sidebars deal with the content of Catholic teaching so we'll all know what we're talking about. God is neither man nor woman, but sometimes you've got to use a pronoun. I've stuck with 'Him' for consistency. When referring to fictional people in examples I've alternated between him and her, so no gender should feel left out. And I use contractions all the time (a big no-no in the textbook world).

I've gone to great lengths to avoid creating a typical Religion textbook, but all those efforts will be pointless and **this book will make no difference in your life if you just read it.** If you don't approach it differently, then, like most books, it will flow in your eyeballs, ricochet through your brain, and vanish when the next input starts arriving.

Don't let this happen. Your faith matters for the long haul and the key to the code will not come up in a Google search if you forget it. So make it stick by getting actively involved. You can:

- Use a rainbow of sticky notes, highlighters or markers to flag things you want to remember.
- Wrestle honestly with the questions provided by yours truly at chapter endings.
- Start a journal on your tablet.
- Get a real-life notebook and pen (gasp) and write, doodle, or draw your thoughts.
- Earmark interesting pages.
- Use smart phone reminders to start some new habits.
- Jot your questions or doubts in the margins.

Most importantly, dare to learn how to pray. Seriously. There's a guide at the end of every chapter. Let yourself feel awkward at the beginning. That's normal. Trust that God will do the work to meet you where you are.

You face big, real-life questions every day, and you need big, real-life answers every day. Whether you're a student in full-time Catholic school, PSR or CCD, or searching on your own, I guarantee that life-altering faith is the key that will decode all of life's gibberish and lead you to the answers.

I'll even go a step further: life-altering faith is seeking you. The key to breaking the code is to let yourself be found.

Peg Dubrowski

Chapter One

Find Your Purpose on the PATH

Check out the timeline of human inventions on this page. It's an awesome litany of creativity, productivity, perseverance, and innovation. And it's a testimony to human potential and possibility, as well as our determination to explore that potential.

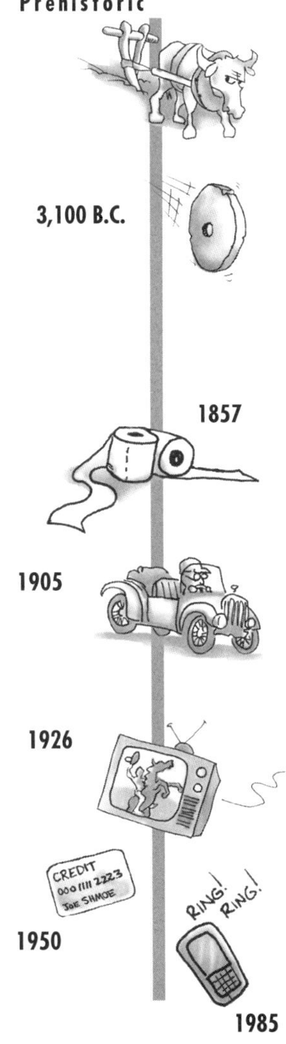

Of course, every invention carries with it built-in hazards or imperfections. Consider the following:

- Cars need fill-ups, oil changes, and replacement parts.
- Credit cards can challenge our powers of self-control.
- Smart phones and computers have driven the pace of daily life into a frenzy of speed and content.
- Texts and tweets are rewriting the rules of grammar and etiquette.

But perhaps the biggest hazard associated with this 'Litany of Inventions' is that it clouds our vision of reality. In some really crucial ways we have gotten ourselves caught up in our own coolness factor. Just look at what we've done! What we've made! What the next 'It' invention might be! We look behind at what we have accomplished, we look ahead at what is possible, and as a species we are overlooking the most important truth: **We did not invent ourselves or invest ourselves with potential.** We cannot take credit for the finest invention: the human being.

The Fundamentals

Everything has a fundamental nature—a basic, truest purpose. **The nature of an object is written into it by its inventor.** For example:

- A chair is a separate seat for one person.
- A car moves people from one place to another.
- A pen writes words on paper.

This seems straight forward enough.

How an item is used, however, can attach a whole different purpose to it. Let's consider that pen, for example:

- You can use the pen to take notes during Geography class.
- You can use the pen to jimmy a locker handle when it's stuck.
- You can use the pen to play darts.
- You can use the pen as a weapon.

True, these are all ways to use that pen, but only the first is the intended purpose of its inventor, Mr. Biro. The others, though perhaps creative, are not a part of the fundamental nature of a pen.

How about that chair?

- You can sit on it during a lecture.
- You can use it as a step stool to get things off the top shelf in your closet.
- You can use it to break open a window when you are involved in a robbery.

Yes, these are all ways to use that chair, but only the first is its intended purpose. As with the pen, some uses diminish the purpose of the object by their outcomes. While you can break open a window with a chair during a robbery, you likely destroy the chair and you surely break a law and commit a sin while doing so. While it may be resourceful to use the pen to jimmy open a stuck locker, it is likely that you will damage the ball point or break the plastic shaft in the process. You are using it for something outside its essential nature.

Conclusions: The chair is most *chair-like* when it's sat upon and the pen is most *pen-like* when we write with it.

What Does That Have to Do with Anything?

Plenty.

Let's consider human beings. Like the chair and the pen, we have a fundamental nature—a basic, truest purpose. Like the chair and the pen, our purpose was defined by our Inventor. Like the chair and the pen, we are most *human-like* when we live out that purpose.

Well then, we best know our fundamental purpose! Check out Psalm 139:13-16 (New American Standard Bible):

You formed my inmost being;
you knit me in my mother's womb,
I praise you, because I am wonderfully made;
wonderful are your works!
My very self you know.
My bones are not hidden from you,
when I was being made in secret,
fashioned in the depths of the earth,
Your eyes saw me unformed.

This text is most likely over 2,700 years old and its author was already giving words to that deep down notion we all feel: there is something much deeper going on than me just walking through the world on my own. There's something inside me nudging me to do the right thing, encouraging me to make a difference, to be an inventor, and to make an impact with my life.

'Knitting' is the visual the psalmist gives us. It brings to mind an old granny, gliding back and forth in her rocker, carefully creating each stitch. Every inch of yarn runs through her fingers as she slowly builds her blanket. God did that with you. Nothing about you is secret or hidden from God. "My very self you know." Think of it! You are completely known and loved by the One who knitted you into being. God tenderly wove you into existence in His own image. And similar to the instruction manual that accompanies every new invention, whether a car, pacemaker, or smart phone, there is an instruction manual that guides your highest and best use, too. It is a manual written on your heart by God, inscribed there during the profound creation of *you.*

An important point: **no two manuals on this earth are the same.** The guys and girls in your classes have their own guides to read, interpret, and follow. That's their work. *Your* work is to find *your* manual and learn all its ins and outs. It will guide you in living out the purpose God has set for you.

Summing it up: You came to this awesome Earth designed by God who:

- Loves you with great passion.
- Decked you out with the potential to impact history in your own time and place.
- Lives within you at all times.
- Is anxious to get started with you on this adventure.

Jesus: Your Compass

God's been working hard to help us understand our purpose throughout history. Ultimately, Jesus came to Earth to *demonstrate* for us our intended purpose. God finally took on a human body to show us how to do human life the way God had intended it to be done.

So what did Jesus do, exactly? What directions did he give us about being human? What lessons can we learn from him? The answers lie in the Gospel stories. Turn to the first page in the book of Matthew, Mark, Luke, or John. You won't need to read very long before you start seeing some patterns surfacing. If you consider how Jesus spent his time being human, you'll see right away what he was suggesting for your life.

Lesson #1: Jesus spent a lot of time keeping in touch with his Father. Over and over, the Bible tells us, "Jesus went off by himself to pray." It didn't matter how busy he was or what else could have filled up his schedule. The first item on his agenda was staying connected to his Father.

A few examples:

When he was 12 years old, a whole group of folks from his town went to visit Jerusalem. He skipped the ride back to Nazareth in favor of hanging out in the temple talking about his Father. This didn't go over so well with Mom and Dad, but it's safe to say they got used to this type of stuff. (Luke 2:29-52)

He spent 40 days with God in the desert before beginning his ministry work. (Matthew 4, Mark 4, Luke 4)

The disciples were used to him going off on his own at the end of the day. After feeding the 5,000, healing the hemorrhaging woman, and calling a demon, Legion, out of a man and casting it into a pig (true story), Jesus went off on his own to be with his Father. He sent the apostles across the Sea of Galilee in a boat while he walked alone around the lake. Unfortunately, this didn't work out for the apostles very well . . . big storm . . . read the story at Matthew 14:22-33.

Even while dying on the cross, Jesus was talking to God. Not whining. Not complaining. Not begging. Not blaming. Instead, his eyes and heart were glued on God.

You choose to spend the most time with the people you love. It was the same with Jesus. It's easy to overemphasize Jesus being divine and underplay the fact that he was truly a man. Just like you, he made choices about who he hung out with and how he spent his time.

Jesus knew the ultimate secret: by making his relationship with the Father Priority #1, he would know if he was on the right path in his daily life. It didn't mean the path would always be easy and fun. Indeed, when the going got tough later in his ministry, Jesus sought out his Father's support and guidance even more. Only by hanging out with God could Jesus find courage and resilience for living out his mission.

That's your first purpose, too: Know and love God, completely and fiercely. Spend time with God. Talk to God. Ask God to show you how to be a better daughter or son. Tell God what's going on with your day. Share your worries and ask for advice. Pour it all out, the good and the bad. And then, *listen.* Pay attention to the messages and guidance you receive. God wants nothing more than to love you by being with you every step of the day and is just waiting for an invitation. (Plenty more about this later. Good relationships take time, effort, commitment, and certain skills. You'll be learning and practicing all of these in the pages ahead.)

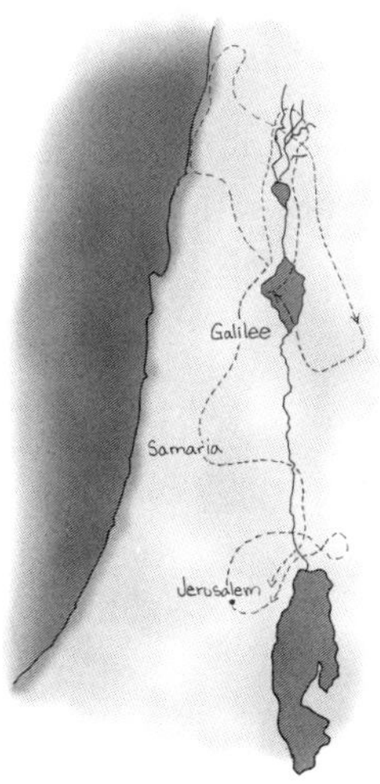

Lesson #2: When not spending time with his Father, Jesus was hanging out with his closest friends, the 12 apostles, and interacting with the folks who started to follow him once his ministry really got underway. He was a traveling preacher and his name spread like wildfire through Judea, Galilee, and even Samaria.

During his years of ministry, Jesus crisscrossed Palestine by boat and foot. As he traveled, he visited the homes of outcasts, hugged lepers, convinced sinners that God loved them enough to forgive any sin, and started conversations with those others ignored. He restored people's vision, raised the dead, called demons out of people possessed, cried with folks who were grieving, and corrected the disciples and the synagogue leaders when they were off the mark. He taught, trained, and guided the disciples to be leaders, relaxed in the homes of his good friends, and responded to every single request for help that was made of him.

Moreover, Jesus taught and showed us that **our second purpose is to be good to other people in God's name.** We do this when we spend our days as he spent his days: loving, healing, helping, comforting, enjoying, guiding, listening and responding to family, friends, acquaintances, and even strangers.

Your Purpose Is to PATH

We can reduce everything about the Gospels and our Catholic faith to these two simple lessons Jesus taught us:

1. Know and love God, completely and fiercely.
2. Be good to other people in God's name.

While that is pretty straightforward, there's even a shorter way to say it: **Be Holy!** Holiness is nothing more than pursuing this first and highest purpose throughout your lifetime. From now on, we're going to refer to this ultimate, God-given purpose as **PATH: P**ursue **A**ll **T**hings **H**oly. In God's design for the universe as a whole, and you in particular, **the plan for you is that you would be holy by knowing and loving God and being good to others in God's name.**

1. Put an X on the following continuums indicating how committed you are to each part of your True Purpose.

Know and love God completely and fiercely.

0% I I I I I 25% I I I I I 50% I I I I I 75% I I I I I 100%

Be good to other people in God's name.

0% I I I I I 25% I I I I I 50% I I I I I 75% I I I I I 100%

2. Which portion of your True Purpose is more challenging to live out?

Pray the Sign of the Cross and then ask Jesus to come and be with you.

Name four people you feel are on the PATH.

What qualities identify each as a person of the PATH?

Thank God for putting each of these four individuals in your life.

Ask God to bless each one of them during this day.

Close with the Sign of the Cross.

Chapter Two

Potential

Potential: something that can develop or become actual; possibility.

The potential in nature is incredible and indescribable. This makes sense since God created everything in nature, and God is incredible and indescribable. We can see this potential all around us. For instance, the seeds from the cone of a giant, coastal redwood tree start out no larger than a kernel of popcorn. Yet the illustration to the right gives you a good sense of the circumference of a typical coastal redwood when it's fully grown.

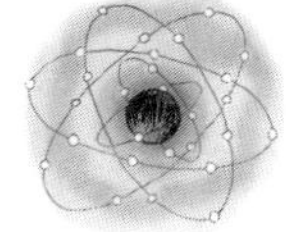

Here's another example. This is a diagram of a plutonium atom, a structure so small that it is invisible to the human eye and detectable only with high-powered microscopes.

It doesn't look like much, but through a process called fission, the nucleus (center) of a plutonium atom can be split open. When that happens, an enormous amount of energy is released. That energy can be used to create...

...electricity in nuclear power plants

...or an atomic bomb.

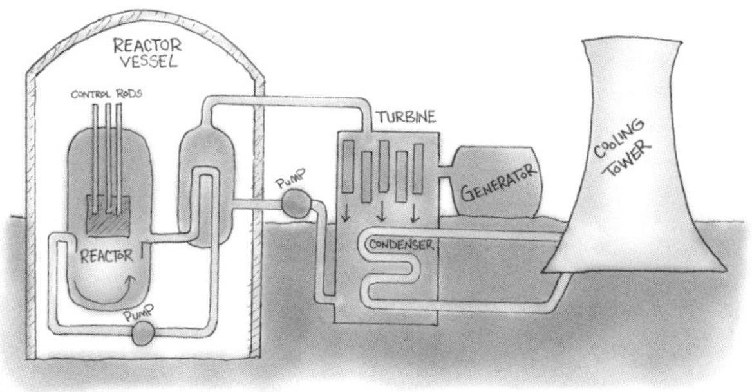

All that potential inside a single, invisible atom.

Potential in Parable

Jesus used his own set of examples from nature to teach about the possibility and potential inside each of us. He wanted to wake us up to our purpose and inspire us to work towards reaching our potential, so he used the parable of the mustard seed. In Matthew 13:31-32, Jesus said:

> *The Kingdom of Heaven is like a mustard seed*
> *that a person took and sowed in a field.*
> *It is the smallest of all seeds, yet when fully grown*
> *it is the largest of plants.*

Your purpose is planted within you, like that mustard seed. You feel it every day when you try to make good choices or when you witness something happening in the locker room that you know isn't right. You help it grow every time you follow its lead by standing up for the person being made fun of or choosing to do chores without being asked.

Let's be clear about what is meant by the **Kingdom of Heaven.** This is pretty simple, actually. It means that **all creation lives out its true purpose as created by God.** So for you and for me, it means that when we know and love God, completely and fiercely, and are good to others in God's name, we are doing our part to create the Kingdom while we are here on Earth.

The most amazing thing about this whole set up is that everyone, though sharing the same fundamental purpose as human beings, will develop his own mustard seed in a different way. That's why we each have our own owner's manual. You may be a teacher, a coach, an accountant, a bank executive, a politician, an astronaut, or a fashion designer. Some of you will be married, some parents, priests, nuns, and some may be single. You may live on a farm, in suburbia, or in one of the busy big cities like New York or L.A. It doesn't matter what you do or where you do it. What matters is that you pursue it with your fundamental purpose front and center. When you pursue your passions, desires, talents, and skills with that purpose guiding you, reaching your potential is guaranteed.

Holiness is nothing more than pursuing your first and highest purpose throughout your lifetime. That's what the saints did. In their own time and place they lived their life with a razor sharp awareness of what it means to know, love, and serve God. They were as crazy different from each other as a rapper is from an opera star. They were kings and paupers, married women and slaves, great thinkers and quiet doers. Some lived in booming metropolises, others lived in caves. Some lived quiet lives and weren't heard of until after they died and their stories began to be told. Some were in the papers and the topic of conversations all throughout their lifetimes. But each dedicated their life to Pursuing All Things Holy, or to the PATH.

Real Lives on the PATH

You may be thinking something similar to the following: *"All this talk of saints and holiness! That's for other people. You know the type: they have no life and never laugh and walk around in outdated clothes with their hands in a perfect steeple fold."*

To which I say: "Aaaaaarrrrggggghhhhh!"

Consider the following folks:

- He visited 129 countries in 25 years, spoke 12 languages, enjoyed jogging, weight training, mountain hiking, football and downhill skiing, shared meals with five American presidents and over 80 world leaders, wrote 16 books, seven plays and three books of poetry, and rose to the highest position of leadership in his chosen field—faith. (Pope St. John Paul II, d. 2005)

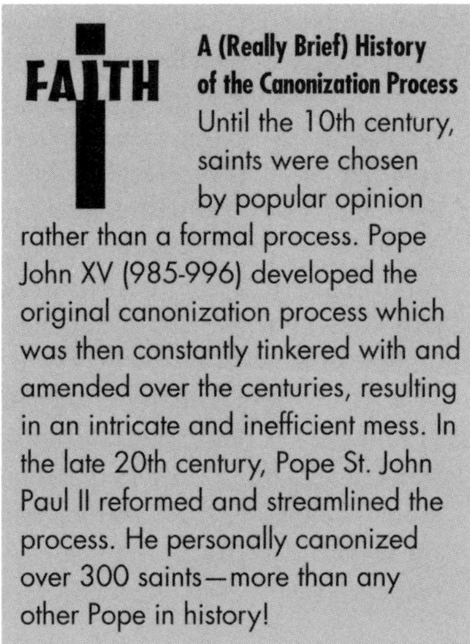

A (Really Brief) History of the Canonization Process

Until the 10th century, saints were chosen by popular opinion rather than a formal process. Pope John XV (985-996) developed the original canonization process which was then constantly tinkered with and amended over the centuries, resulting in an intricate and inefficient mess. In the late 20th century, Pope St. John Paul II reformed and streamlined the process. He personally canonized over 300 saints—more than any other Pope in history!

- She was married to a successful businessman and the mother of five children when the rug was pulled out from under her. Her husband contracted a deadly disease and couldn't beat it. Over time she was left a penniless widow. She converted to Catholicism and, while still raising her own children, founded a religious order dedicated to running schools and orphanages for the huge population of immigrants coming to America in the early 1800s. (St. Elizabeth Ann Seton, d. 1821)

- As an English aristocrat, he rose steadily through the ranks of politics, starting out as a representative and ultimately becoming the Speaker of the House of Commons. He was the King's closest advisor and friend, often representing him on diplomatic missions throughout Europe. He was happily married, raised four children, and owned several homes throughout England. (St. Thomas More, d. 1535)
- She rose from poor farm girl to leader of a nation's army. Her bold passion, creative strategies, and bravery led the French army in winning back almost half of the territory England had conquered from them. Enemy leaders feared her so much that they laid down their arms peacefully rather than go to battle against her and her army. You go, girl! (St. Joan of Arc, d. 1431)
- These twin brothers and doctors are believed to have pioneered the procedure of transplanting (back in the 200's, no less!) by grafting a donated leg onto an amputee. They were known for experimenting with many unorthodox, but highly effective, forms of treatment. And they never accepted payment for their service, preferring instead to work for the glory of God. (Sts. Cosmos and Damian, d. 287)
- She lived in a society completely dominated by men, but did not let anyone tell her who to marry or how to live. She turned away suitor after suitor (even the Governor), refusing their gifts and promises

The Modern Canonization Process

Step 1: A Bishop assembles vital information about a candidate's cause for sainthood and sends it to the Vatican. Theologians and Cardinals study the information and determine if the individual is irrefutably virtuous.

Step 2: Upon this group's recommendation, the Pope declares the individual "Venerable," or a good role model.

Step 3: Beatification is the next rung on the ladder to sainthood and requires proof of a miracle attributed to the individual after his or her death. Once the miracle is confirmed the title of "Blessed" is bestowed on the individual. (Cool fact: martyrs do not need proof of miracles. Having the courage and strength to make the ultimate sacrifice for one's faith is miracle enough!)

Step 4: A date for canonization to sainthood can be set once a second miracle attributed to the candidate is validated.

> of wealth, eventually withstanding mockery, cruel shaming, and grisly torture when these men were embarrassed to find themselves rejected by 'a girl'. But she knew she was called to something much more. (St. Agnes, d. 304)

Doctor, lawyer, parent, farmer, priest, teenager—it doesn't matter what your circumstance. If you allow it, God will work with you to create the Kingdom. And here's the simple truth: **if you don't pursue your first and highest purpose you will not, in fact, find true happiness** in this one life you have to live.

Plenty of folks pursue likes and followers, novel experiences, and value friends and family among all else. The hottest fashions, footwear and smartphones are billion dollar markets because desires lead to spending. But will any of this lead to true happiness? Nope. Sure, you'll feel happy when you view your inbox, enjoy a family party, or check yourself out in a mirror and see that you are looking fine, but none of these will last. You'll start longing for something else, someone else, the next best experience, or something trendier. It's just the truth about being human. Pursuing stuff, followers, relationships, and status for their own sake *never* leads to true happiness because it's not a part of the Grand Design. But *it is* a part of our struggle with free will and realizing that choosing God's will is, ultimately, the road to happiness.

Summing it up: If the goals you set for yourself are not deeply hooked into knowing and loving God and being good to other folks, you'll find an eerily empty, creepily unfulfilled hole right smack in the middle of your soul. Not pretty.

Are You on the PATH or Are You LOST? That Is the Question.

Given this reality, why do so few people PATH—**P**ursue **A**ll **T**hings **H**oly? Why are so many of us LOST—**L**etting **O**ther **S**tuff **T**riumph? What's *really* going on is that people are either developing their potential as made in God's image or they're not. This is a *choice,* not something that is forced upon us.

All people are in one of three stages of potential. As you read about them, ask yourself which stage you are in.

Stage One: Unaware and Uninformed

You don't know what is possible when you hook your life up with Jesus. You are spending so much time listening to false messages and distractions that you haven't heard the Good News. Your potential is pretty much inert.

Stage Two: Aware But Unequipped or Undecided

You've heard the news. You sense that God is calling you to something, but you don't have a map or the tools for the task and you don't want to put forth the effort to acquire them. Ummm . . . you're lazy.

Stage Three: Aware and Exploring

Your potential is exploding. You get it. You've experienced The Grand Design inside yourself and accept the challenge of pursuing it. You've decided to hit the road and are acquiring the tools needed to make the journey successful. You know it's work and you know it's worth it.

I call the first two stages LOST and the third stage the PATH. There's a whole slew of skills, tools, and choices that belong to those on the PATH. They are like the suitcase we carry in the trunk and the GPS we follow from wake-up to bedtime. They are what the rest of this book is about. Learn them, practice them, and make a commitment to them and your PATH will take you to authentic happiness.

Wired for the PATH

This is the Great News: **your purpose is to Be Holy and to PATH. It is why you were made.** It is the plan for you because you have been made in God's image and God is All That Is Holy. You carry within you the seed of holiness, and are designed to nurture that seed to its full potential. If you let yourself get caught up in that thought and follow where it leads, then wow! Your future is tremendously exciting.

While all Catholics have the potential to become saints who PATH, it seems that very few (a) believe they can or (b) know how to do it. Concrete tools will help you on this adventure into discipleship. You'll begin learning and working with them in the pages ahead. On the other hand, some real roadblocks exist (self-doubt, false beliefs, temptation, lack of awareness) and you will begin recognizing and eliminating them. Over time you will explore this wiring, learn how it works and how to use it to build up the Kingdom of God within yourself, your family, in your school, and in all areas of your life.

1. Which stage of potential are you in?
2. How willing are you to begin pursuing the PATH?
3. Who brings out the best, most PATH-like version of you?

Pray the Sign of the Cross and then ask Jesus to come and be with you.

Reread the following sentence a few times: "Very few Catholics (a) believe they can be saints or (b) know how to do it."

Which part of the sentence applies more to you, (a) or (b)?

Talk to Jesus about this call to sainthood and how you are challenged by it. Don't worry about what you say or how you say it. Just be honest and open. Know that he is overjoyed that you want to talk about this.

After sharing your thoughts, sit with Jesus for a few moments. Let him enjoy your company. Let yourself be comfortable in his presence.

As you close your prayer, thank him and let him know you'll be back to talk with him later.

Close with the Sign of the Cross.

Chapter Three

Happiness

Consider what makes you happy. Seriously. Consider it right now. I'll wait.

• • • • • • •

Being happy is the #1 motivator behind your choices and mine. Feeling happy, in big or small ways, carries a lot of weight in every choice and decision we make. A few examples:

- When ordering at Taco Bell, you choose what you're craving and it's great.
- When dressing for a mixer at school, you choose an outfit that gives you confidence.
- When considering high school or college, you'll choose the one that is the best 'fit'.
- When a guy asks a girl out on a date, he thinks he'll like hanging out with her and that she'll say yes.

Whether Pursuing All Things Holy (PATH) or on the road to Letting Other Stuff Triumph (LOST), everyone wants to *be happy.* But as you might guess, significant differences exist between how a person on the PATH and a person who is LOST find happiness. It's a pretty important difference. In fact, it's a difference that defines everything about them and their lifetime.

LOST Happiness: Other Stuff

Those who are Letting Other Stuff Triumph believe they will find happiness in just that: Other Stuff. It might be the latest cut of jeans, or the newest smart phone, or even getting a rise out of classmates when acting like the class clown. Having an enormous number of Instagram followers does it for some folks. Good grades, receiving compliments for a nice singing voice, or recognition for superior athletic skills brings happiness to others. Some find happiness in figuring out how to do the absolute minimum to get by in a situation, while others experience it as the result of hard work and perseverance. The point here is that **happiness in the Land of the LOST is dependent on stuff outside of its citizens.** It can be worn, liked, touched, hashtagged, followed, bought, achieved, and purchased.

All of this presents an obvious dilemma: *external things can change.* A new, smarter phone comes on the market, classmates grow bored with your antics, your GPA dips, the new kid at school sings better, you're injured on the field, a new Social Media outlet sends you back to the drawing board collecting friends and admirers, underachieving leads to mediocrity, and overachieving leads to perfectionism. **Once something changes out there you have to go seeking your happiness in something else.**

All of this time spent finding happiness when you are LOST can exhaust a person!

PATH Happiness: Gratitude for the Gift

On the flip side, people on the PATH find happiness in one place and one place alone. It doesn't move around on them, take different forms, or slip out of their hands. It is steady, constant, and firm.

Happiness on the PATH is defined by two beliefs:

Belief #1: God loved me into life.
You didn't call yourself into being, structure your DNA, or make yourself unlike anyone else. That's all God. This sounds obvious, but in our crazy, fast-paced world we can easily go through a whole day, week or month forgetting that without God's handiwork we wouldn't be here in the first place. Yet, this is the front and center thought of people on the PATH! **They know they owe their existence to God.** They want to say: "Thanks."

TRUE TALES

A wonderful priest at my home parish worked a favorite line into every homily he gave. Out of the blue he would suddenly say, "Raise your hand if the first thing you did when you woke up this morning was to say, 'Hey, thanks God for another day!'" (I've got to admit that there were more than a few times that I could not honestly raise my hand because I was so caught up in the busy-ness of my life.)

Belief #2: I show my thanks for this amazing life by dedicating the gifts, talents, and desires God gave me to His Grand Design.
God doesn't want payment for this gift of life. God just wants you to use it for all it is intended to be. As a Catholic, this is what you are called to believe about your existence: God conceived you and formed you and breathed His very own life into you. Reread that sentence. (Do it.) When you live your life creating the best you possible, a part of God is revealed to all of us. **That's why you were created: to make God's glory and holiness visible to others through your life.**

This is the will of God: your holiness.
1 Thessalonians 4:3

When you accept that God loved you into life, you realize that true happiness can only be found in loving and serving God in all that you do by following the PATH, whether that's on a soccer field, in a tech lab, at the dinner table, or in your career. The best part is that this is all within your control, because the desire and determination to PATH exists within you.

Nothing out there can change the truth: you have been built for holiness.

Choose the PATH, Choose Your Purpose

Time to bring back the chair and the pen. Remember, they too have a fundamental purpose that was given to them by their inventor. But completely unlike the chair and the pen and every other thing in this world, humans choose whether or not to live out their purpose. A chair does not sit upon itself or throw itself through a window, nor does a pen lunge itself at a dartboard or feverishly write down a teacher's thoughts. No, they have to be acted on. Humans, however, are both object and actor. **We decide what purpose we are going to pursue. That's free will in action.** For example:

- You can make having the right connections your primary motivation —on the Web, at school, at work in the future.
- You can enjoy as many experiences as you can fit into your budget and your schedule.
- You can decide you will be a multi-millionaire and orchestrate your choices to get yourself there.
- You can spend your days obsessing over every detail of your body—hair, weight, lip size, fashion.
- You can dedicate yourself to knowing and loving God, completely and fiercely, and serving God by being good to others in His name.

Think back to the outcomes for the pen and the chair when they were used for some purpose other than what they were made for: mistreated, wasted, and perhaps broken. What follows, therefore, is pretty obvious. If you decide to pursue some goal other than loving God and being good to others in God's name, your life's outcome is super sketchy. You will not realize your potential. You will find yourself broken and burdened in all sorts of unexpected ways. You will be disconnected from your true self and that never results in happiness.

By living a life on the PATH, we come to know and love God and, in the end, we realize God's desire for us and experience true happiness. The only other option is to Let Other Stuff Triumph, and there's plenty that can knock us off course. We need to learn how to keep to the PATH by recognizing which roads lead to holiness.

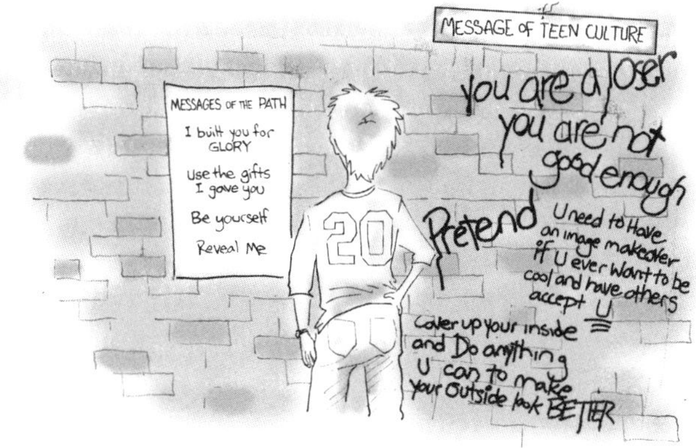

1. What *stuff* (followers, status, money, success, reputation, friendship, fashion, stress, expectations) leads you to be LOST some days?

2. List a subject you like, a talent you have, and an activity you are involved in. Brainstorm ways you can be good to others in God's name while you are involved in each.

Pray the Sign of the Cross and then ask Jesus to come and be with you.

Think about the talent you wrote about in #2 above. Identify a positive memory you have of yourself using that talent.

Close your eyes and recall this memory in as much detail as possible. See yourself, your surroundings, and the others present. Place yourself in the memory and visualize it as best as you can.

Ask God to show you how you were or could have been good to others in His name during the experience. Be patient and open to God's wisdom.

Finally, thank God for this powerful memory and insight.

End with the Sign of the Cross.

Chapter Four

Road Trip

Imagine a cross-country vacation in the U.S.A. You're going to see all the highlights from New York to L.A., Chicago to Dallas, and everything in between.

Now imagine packing for this trip. You'd be seeing weather of all types and terrain of all sorts, so a variety of clothes and footwear would be crucial. You'd eat all kinds of food, interact with tourists from all over the world on holiday in America, and stay in an endless variety of hotels. You'd put thousands and thousands of miles on your car and it would probably start smelling a little like humans after not too long. You'd have to trust your GPS and brush up your map-reading skills for the times when your GPS can't see the satellite. Then there's all that seat time in the car between destinations. How will you avoid boredom? Plus, it's pretty much inevitable that something, if not many somethings, will go wrong. You'll have to problem solve on the spot or be flexible enough to alter your plan. But in the end, if you planned enough and were flexible enough, this would be the vacation of a lifetime.

All the ups and downs of a cross-country vacation apply to life, whether you are on the PATH or LOST. On either route, you'll find:

- Many settings and backgrounds
- Lots of people moving in and out of your pathway
- Times when life is dull and you feel discontent
- Experiences that take your breath away
- Instances when you realize you are underprepared
- Numerous unexpected small glitches to manage
- Occasional high and tight curve balls that find you diving for the dirt
- Perhaps even a life-altering catastrophe

Most of us would spend many weeks preparing for a cross-country vacation—

plotting a course, gathering maps, reading travel blogs, shopping, tying up loose ends at home, and packing. If we would do all of this for a vacation, it would seem pretty logical that we need to do even more to ready ourselves for 70+ years of being on the PATH. A lifetime journey seeking God's will requires you hit the road with a well-packed suitcase.

Packing for the PATH

Each of us has a suitcase we take through life. You have a variety of items in yours already. Some of them you seem born with. And you know what, you were. Whether it's singing, athletics, drama, math, building, playing with children, or tracking animals while hunting, you've got some concrete skills in your suitcase already. They were given to you by God. Chances are good that God desires you to use them in your pursuit of happiness. They are like breadcrumbs strewn for you to follow on your way to realizing the purpose intended for you.

You may also have some items in your suitcase that are more spiritual in nature. In fact, the Church calls these the Moral Virtues. While you can't fold them and you don't need to worry about them wrinkling, it is crucial that you eventually fill your suitcase with these essential virtues. They are 'weather appropriate' no matter what the weather, and they will help you traverse all sorts of terrain, wherever the PATH may take you.

What to Bring

Stuff I Got	Stuff I Need
motivation	patience
Common sense	self-discipline
energy	courage
Creativity	empathy
	tact
	temperance

So, what's a moral **virtue**? It is any attitude or frame of mind that directs you to the PATH by enabling you to opt for doing the holy, God-seeking thing in any given situation. Virtues do this by managing your thoughts and actions. **They help you control what's going on inside so that you can respond effectively to what's going on outside of you.** They are the stepping stones to knowing and loving God and serving God by being good to others. Furthermore, they serve you in every other area of your life as well. Virtues enable you to be a better student, a better friend, and a better parent and employee down the road.

How Do I Get Moral Virtues?

Of course, they don't do this magically, though sometimes we really wish it worked that way. We'd like to just pull in to the nearest Virtue Drive-thru

and order up a double order of patience when irritation with the little bro is out of control. Or, how about a mega-size of self-control when it's 2:20 and the teacher is still lecturing after a day filled with lectures? Nope. Virtues are earned and acquired.

Every once in a while I'm going to throw in a direct quote from the *Catechism of the Catholic Church.* It's the ultimate textbook of Catholic teaching, pretty lengthy, and maybe parts of it are a little over your head right now. But, just like the Bible, you can definitely understand it if you put in the effort needed.

> The virtuous person is one "who freely practices the good."
> (Catholic Church, 1804)

The Catechism is telling you that total and complete responsibility for the acquisition of virtues is in your hands. **By your free will you choose to work on collecting these personal power sources.** By your free will you decide to master the things that might tempt you to diverge off the PATH. By your free will you keep your eyes on the target, which is, in the words of St. Paul, "The prize of God's upward call." (Philippians 3:14)

That's *The Prize,* folks: God's upward call. You hear it in your heart and in your soul. You feel called to something good and true and significant. There's a voice deep inside affirming that, "Yes, dude. There's something important you have to do for me." *That's* the upward call. Everyone's is different and **your task in life is to hear God's voice and discern what you are asked to do.** Virtues are the tools that will enable you to hear and follow that call.

In review, here's what we know about the Virtues:

- God doesn't plant them in you; it's up to you to secure them for the trip.
- Anyone can secure them through practice, dedication and self-discipline.
- Securing them is the absolute key to pursuing your upward call.

So start filling your suitcase!

TRUE TALES

I taught guitar to seventh graders for many years. Some of those kids came into my classroom and bingo! They could play. It all made sense to them: the reading of the music, the eye/hand coordination, and the technical skills. They were meant to be guitar players. I was always blown away by their gift. But I was even more blown away by the students who struggled with their limitations and succeeded anyway. Maybe they were never the best guitar players, but because they pursued virtues in the classroom (self-discipline, positive attitude, perseverance) they could put a guitar in their suitcase by the end of the semester, right next to some lifelong virtues.

Catholicism 101: The Cardinal Virtues

There are four virtues that carry the name **Cardinal Virtues**. They are **the four central moral virtues of our faith.** Each one of them has a series of other virtues and attributes that support it, something akin to spokes on a wheel giving strength to the hub in the center of the wheel. The more supporting characteristics you build up, the stronger your Cardinal Virtue will become. As you can see from the chart below, we are talking about some powerhouse qualities.

Build Your VQ

Prudence	Justice	Fortitude	Temperance
focus	caring	confident	chastity
good judgment	compassion	hard-working	moderation
logic	cooperation	honor	modesty
organization	generosity	humor	obedience
perceptive	kindness	loyal	patience
reflective	mercy	motivation	purity
time management	respect	perserverance	responsibility
understanding	self-sacrifice	resilent	self-control
wisdom	tact	risk-taking	simplicity

For now, let's just concentrate on the four Cardinal Virtues and be sure we are clear on what each one means.

1. **Prudence:** The ability to look at any situation and recognize correctly what is right and what is wrong, what is good or evil.

   If you are prudent, you know how to make wise decisions and wise judgments. You know it's best to prepare for that test, rather than face the temptation to cheat. You recognize when a friend's bad-mouthing of a teacher is not something you should participate in. If you are prudent, you can take your own personal will out of the picture and ask God to give you the right perspective in any situation.

2. **Fortitude:** Having the strength and courage to do what needs to be done in the face of obstacles.

   So you really, really don't like Spanish, but you're doing well in class anyway because you work hard and are overcoming the temptation to do *anything* (sleep, eat, text) but study Spanish. Or, you kept out of the gossip that was going around about someone even though there was some making fun of you by your friends as a result. You are developing the virtue of fortitude.

3. **Justice:** Having genuine concern and desire for each person's right to be respected and working hard to think and act honorably towards others.

   That's a mouthful, but it's a pretty basic concept. For instance, you just can't let someone take the fall for you in class if a teacher wrongly identifies who was causing the ruckus (that would be you). You can't use them that way. It would eat you up inside. On a larger scale, when a guest speaker who runs schools in poor countries came

to your Church, you decided to sponsor a student yourself. You knew it meant you'd have to do extra chores or more babysitting to cover the cost, but that kid should have an opportunity for a solid education. These are examples of justice in action.

4. **Temperance:** Having control over your impulses, instincts, and passions. It's really about being able to say "No" to yourself and mean it.

   On a very simple level, if you are temperate you can actually eat one portion of Cheetos from a freshly opened bag (the author struggles here!). At a much more developed level, you are able to make a commitment of chastity to yourself, your future spouse, and God, and you will follow through on that commitment.

   Temperance is all about moderation, and it's a tough one in our culture of excess and instant everything. Many of us are convinced that we need a pair of shoes for every outfit (okay, maybe not the guys) or the newest version of the iPhone the day it comes out. Saying "No" to yourself also means saying "No" to the clamor of voices bubbling up from the Internet, advertisements and peers.

Your Upward Call

People who are on the PATH are, in fact, different from folks who are LOST. How? Easy answers are tempting: "They're lucky" or "They've got it all going for them" or "They were born smarter or more talented." But the easy answers are just not true. People who are Pursuing All Things Holy differ from those LOST in one significant way: **they've decided to work from the inside out to fashion the most virtuous rendition of themselves that they can muster.** They've *decided* to do this by following God's will for them, knowing this will lead them to live to their full potential. They've *decided* to trust that God will be their strength, even occasionally offering a push in the right direction, as they develop the virtues needed for a lifetime on the PATH. In the end, their lives will be deeply purposeful and wildly effective. With St. Paul, they commit themselves to the Inside Job and the Upward Call. They've *decided* to take the route he urged in his letter to the Philippians, 4:8:

> *Whatever is true, whatever is honorable, whatever is just,*
> *whatever is pure, whatever is lovely, whatever is gracious,*
> *if there is any excellence, and if there is anything worthy of praise,*
> *think about these things.*

1. Reflect on how well you have developed the Cardinal Virtues and rank them from strongest to weakest: prudence, fortitude, justice, temperance.

2. List several adults or older teens you know who exhibit each Cardinal Virtue. Try not to repeat names.

Pray the Sign of the Cross and ask Jesus to be with you.

Reread the closing Bible verse of this chapter several times. Which of the first six phrases most captures your attention?

Keeping the phrase you selected in mind, close your eyes and think of all the people or things that fit this description.

When you are done, thank God for all of these.

Close with the Sign of the Cross.

CHAPTER FIVE

The Inside Job

You live in two different worlds.

Your first world involves everything that happens outside of the skin that holds you in place. It is the realm of other people, schedules and deadlines, social media, and entertainment. It's the Spanish class you attend, the part time job you hold down, and the fact that your dinner has mushrooms in it and they make you want to vomit. Get it? This world is Out There.

The second world is the one inside your skin and its power source lies between your ears. You have about five quarts of blood in your veins and arteries and that blood travels about 12,000 miles each day and you have biological processes going on inside you about which you are clueless. This is all very cool, but scientists have learned that the organ sitting inside your noggin is at the helm of all this incessant interior activity. The brain, fellow PATH travelers, is the most promising-yet-underdeveloped apparatus known to mankind. Deep within its recesses it carries the codes for keeping the rest of what's inside your skin working correctly. It is the hub of all learning, communication, feelings, decision making, creativity, problem solving, humor, and all things human. Ultimately, the brain is the channel through which you and God connect on the Inside.

Like a reflex that just happens, people of the PATH have an immediate reaction of, "That's it!" when they consider the Inside. They know that what happens Inside is within their strike zone of impact. They can't change their Spanish teacher's personality, make flipping burgers more interesting, or miraculously have mushrooms fly off the plate, but they can control how they react to their Spanish teacher, their attitude towards flipping patties, and what they do about those mushrooms.

Working on the Inside Improves the Outside

What percentage of your overall happiness is tied to the world Out There and what percentage is tied to the Inside?

- When you are on the PATH, you know that *90% of your happiness is rooted in what you do Inside* and only 10% is linked to what's happening Out There.
- When you are LOST, you believe the exact opposite: *90% of your happiness is rooted in what happens Out There* and only 10% is linked to what's happening Inside.

In a nutshell, when we are LOST we are forgetting the most basic of facts: we have been given no control over what happens Out There. **All the power and control we have been given by God is located on the Inside.** When we are on the PATH, we are striving to exert that power and control, learning how to shape our days, our choices, and our perspectives from the inside out with God as our co-pilot.

You are powerful because God has made you and walks with you. With God as your constant companion and Voice of Truth, you can shape your Inside into that amazing and marvelous piece of creation that God has in store. Then, no matter what you walk through Out There you can hold on to peace and happiness on the Inside.

The Law of 90/10 is the ultimate responsible thinking strategy. With 90/10 we eliminate our role as victims of the world Out There by championing the much bigger belief:

"I have the strength for everything through him who empowers me."
Philippians 4:13

Yoke It Up

How do we know we can do all things through Christ who strengthens us? Because *Jesus told us we can,* of course. In the Gospel of Matthew, Jesus said:

Take my yoke upon you and learn from me, for I am meek
and humble of heart; and you will find rest for yourselves.
For my yoke is easy, and my burden light.
Matthew 11:28-30

Clear as mud, right? How many of us know anything about yokes, or oxen, or farming? Ninety-eight percent of us live in cities or suburbia. Even if we are farmers, we use combines and tractors. An important lesson here: if you don't get the Bible, ask questions. It's really worth the effort to learn a little bit about the context and content of its stories because then you can say, "Oh. I get it!" So, let's do a little research about these things, otherwise we just let our 21st century way of thinking get in the way.

Here are some 1st Century farming tidbits you didn't know about:

- Yokes were made of wood and fitted to the particular ox; as the ox grew, new yokes were made to fit.
- A well-fitted yoke was comfortable, not irritating, like a good pair of shoes.
- When its natural power was harnessed with a yoke, an ox could work harder and produce more. Left to its own devices it crushed stuff and basically wreaked havoc in the field.
- Normally two oxen were yoked side by side.
- With the yoke, the ox was able to do something it could not accomplish alone—be productive and even play a role in producing its own food.

As long as the yoke fit, this was a fulfilling way to spend a day, as oxen go: get some exercise, provide your future meals, and please your owner who cares for your every need.

Okay, with our context in place let's re-read that Bible passage:

Take my yoke upon you and learn from me,
for I am meek and humble of heart;
and you will find rest for yourselves.
For my yoke is easy, and my burden light.
Matthew 11:28-30

Jesus is inviting you to get into his yoke which will be well-fitted and comfortable, not irritating. It will allow you to do things you could never do when left to your own devices and it will keep you from making mistakes as well. He's promising you that your life will be productive and fruitful if you do this. You will create a life-sustaining product if you take on his yoke.

Where, exactly, is Jesus in this yoke metaphor? Let's consider two options:

- **Option #1:** Jesus holds the reins of your yoke. He is your kind and caring master, helping to steer you clear of ruts and rocks, focusing your energies, and helping you to be as effective as possible on the Inside. With him as your guide you can unleash your potential.
- **Option #2:** Jesus is that other ox in the yoke with you. He's right next to you. He's plowed these fields before and knows where the ruts and rocks are. You can follow his lead with confidence. Yoked with him you will unleash your potential on the Inside because he will show you the way.

Whichever way you choose to unpack this little story, you realize that Jesus is committing himself to help you every step of the PATH. **He will help you do the Inside Job of taking control of your thinking and perspective, helping you find his power and your happiness on the Inside.** He's there with you. You just need to open your eyes and ears and get out in the field with him.

Blaming and Excuse Making

Living the Law of 90/10 while on the PATH is not only exciting and liberating, it is also difficult. It takes constant effort to avoid the roads that lead us to be LOST Out There. Two habits in particular need to be broken if we intend to make the transition to 90/10 with the least amount of detours:

1. **The Blame Thrower.** Placing blame is an attempt to protect ourselves, but it only appears to reduce the impact of our negative experiences. In reality, blaming allows what is Out There to sink its hooks into us ever more deeply.

   Rather than moving *beyond* difficulty by exercising our internal strength, we get stuck in it by turning ourselves into victims. Sadly, a great number of adults have never learned to holster this weapon, preferring to spew anger and resentment over taking personal responsibility for their happiness.

2. **The Excuse Shield.** When we forget about 90/10, we can use excuses like shields to deflect responsibility from ourselves. Like the Blame

Thrower, the Excuse Shield also backfires. Trying to protect ourselves by making excuses is a surefire way to remain stuck and at the mercy of what is Out There. Rather than harnessing the strength we have on the Inside, we allow ourselves to become victims by surrendering our personal power at the feet of all that we cannot control.

The Big Shift

You've spent your life learning lessons from and following the directions of other people. You haven't had the skills or ability to care for yourself, so parents and guardians have cared for you, with the help of extended family, teachers, and faith leaders. But during your early teen years an awesome change begins to take place within you. You might experience it as wanting more independence and choosing to hang out with your friends more often. Maybe you find yourself disagreeing with your teacher during an important discussion in your classroom. You might be paying attention to the news and wonder why the world seems so screwed up and what you can do about it.

These are indicators of The Big Shift. It's taking place in your brain. An *explosion* of brain development takes place during your teens and into your early twenties. Your ability to learn will never be greater than it is during this critical decade. More importantly, you will develop skills that are signatures of adulthood: self-control, wise decision making, empathy, and impulse control. **The Big Shift refers to the maturing of your brain and the new skills you can acquire as a result.** This process will prepare you to take the reins of responsibility for your life from your parents and hold them confidently in your own hands.

Ultimately, the fact that you are approaching or have already begun The Big Shift is the best news ever. Really. It means that the choice to PATH and the power to be successful are sitting in the palm of your hands. You get to decide where the road ahead is going to lead and how you are going to navigate it.

No one is pulling your strings or deciding for you. There is nothing that can keep you from reaching your potential if you are determined to attain it by shaping your Inside while in the yoke with Jesus.

The flip side is that there's no one you can blame if you find yourself LOST (Letting Other Stuff Triumph). You'll know you're on the edge of LOST when you are tempted to act like a victim, point fingers, cut corners and make excuses, or whine about how unfair something is Out There.

The amazing instrument sitting between your ears presents a profound responsibility. Learning to form your Inside by living the Law of 90/10 is the cornerstone to accepting that responsibility.

PATH Beliefs	LOST Beliefs
God built me for holiness	I look for happiness outside myself
God and I work together	I'm on my own
We shape my life from the inside out	I wait for the outside to change
I control my thoughts, feelings and behaviors	I am a victim of events and situations
I see choices	I'm stuck
My power comes from the inside	Life is out of my control

1. Which do you prefer: (a) Jesus holds the reins of the yoke or (b) Jesus is the other ox in the yoke with you? Why did you choose this option?

2. Identify an Out There situation about which you have little or no control. Examine yourself. How are you using the Excuse Shield in this situation? Are you blaming someone about this situation?

Pray the Sign of the Cross and then ask Jesus to come and be with you.

Draft a tweet to Jesus. Include any questions and reactions you have regarding getting in the yoke with him. Count your characters.

When completed, offer your tweet as a prayer and spend some time in silence. Believe that he has heard and will respond.

Close with the Sign of the Cross.

Chapter Six

The Frame: Think-Feel-Do-Get

We've established that people of the PATH and people who are LOST are all looking for happiness. They want to get the most out of life, achieve all that they are able to achieve, and attain the things that are important to them—solid relationships, good health, success in school and work. This is the basic purpose of the journey and whether we PATH or are LOST, we're all trying to read the road map of life correctly to find our way there.

Those on the PATH have taken the time to do some extra preparation for the trip. They understand the Law of 90/10 and that the trip can only be successful if they are yoked to Jesus. A well-stocked Road Trip Survival Kit helps them do the Inside Job and develop a deep, real, life-changing relationship with God. Most importantly, they know how to use each item in their kit.

The Frame is the Super Power of the Inside Job. You use it by starting in the Upper Left Corner (ULC) and working your way around it in a clockwise fashion. What the Frame suggests is that:

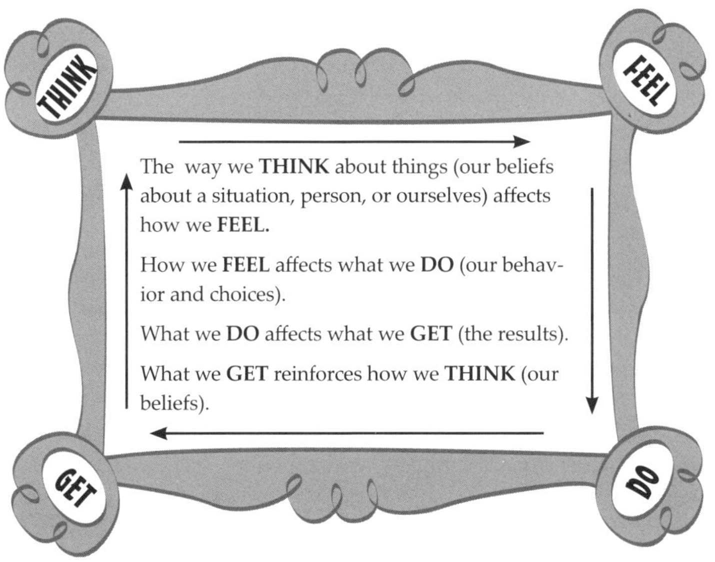

So, if you are getting what you want to be getting in a situation or relationship, you should keep doing what you are doing and keep thinking what you are thinking in that particular instance. Your Frame is working.

Sometimes you'll find yourself in a situation where you are not getting what you want to be getting. You're not getting the grade you want in English. Your best friend seems to be ignoring you. Your relationship with your parents is pretty tense. In these cases, what can you do to increase the chances of getting what is important to you (a better grade, a stronger friendship, peace in your house)? How can you work the Frame to shake up what's going on? That will depend on whether you are on the PATH or LOST.

Options of Those LOST

If you aren't getting the desired outcome in a situation and you are on the road to LOST, you see these options:

1. **Do nothing.** You can just keep on keeping on, thinking the same thoughts and trying the same strategies you are using. Though the track record suggests this will change nothing, it is easy and it is safe because you know what the outcome is and no new risks are involved. This particular choice results in insanity! Isn't it insane to expect different results if you continue to *think* and *do* the same thing?

2. **Change what you FEEL.** So you are getting a low grade in your English class. Just don't feel angry or embarrassed or upset by it. Let it roll off your back. Or, push those negative feelings deep down inside somewhere and replace them with other more positive feelings. These options are impossible, unhealthy, and lead to a troubling disconnect between what is really going on in your life and how you tend to it. Since you basically stuff the problem at hand, eventually the pressure will cause you to erupt, usually inflicting some kind of damage on an innocent bystander.

3. **Change what you DO.** When your younger brother interrupts you for the fourth time while you are on the phone and you have lost all patience with him, just smile at him lovingly and ask the person on the phone if you can talk later because you need to tend to the little one. NOT. This option is totally unrealistic. If you don't first change the *thinking* part of the process, your replacement actions will be fake, difficult, and nothing but a hateful chore. I wouldn't want to be your little brother.

4. Blame someone else for your problem. The Blame Thrower is definitely a fan favorite. People who are LOST almost always leave fingerprints of blame when they are not getting what they want in a situation. They blame the teacher for that English grade and they blame their parents for making them babysit that little brother. They blame the ref for the close loss and they blame their boss when they are fired.

Options on the PATH

If you aren't getting what you want in a particular situation (English class) or relationship (that little brother) and you are on the PATH, you have the power of the Frame at your disposal because you have figured out the key to using it. You don't start with how you feel or what you do. You always begin by taking yourself to the Upper Left Corner (ULC, from now on). **What you think in any given situation is the power behind everything else happening in the system.**

An example will help reveal the power of the Frame. Imagine that your English teacher has assigned you to read a play by Shakespeare. The way you think about this assignment will likely make a difference in the results you get. If you think it will be difficult and a waste of time, your frame will look like this:

If, however, you approach reading Shakespeare as a challenging and worthwhile new experience, your frame will look different.

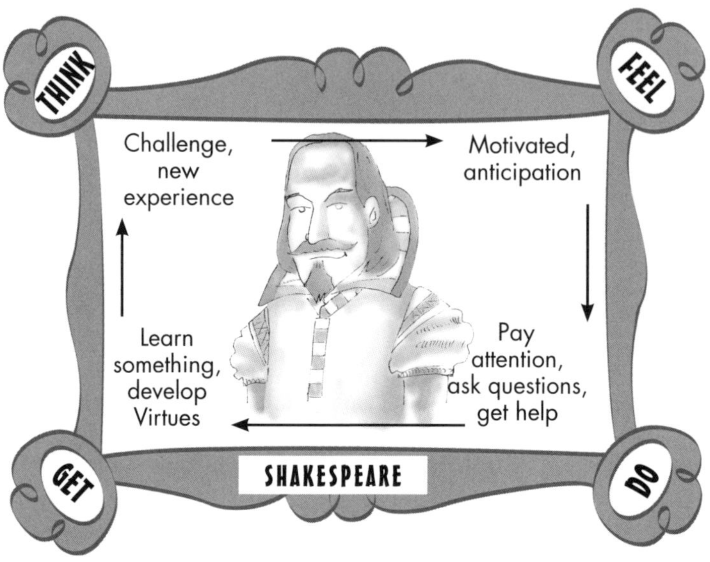

The Frame can help you achieve positive results in any given situation, but it is even more powerful if used while you are in the yoke. **To dramatically increase the effectiveness of the Frame, invite Jesus to come stand in that ULC with you.** Then, just run your thinking by him and see what he thinks. Seriously. It works every time.

EXAMPLE

You are at your wits end with this little brother scenario. These are your thoughts: "Seriously, four times he's interrupted. He's an obnoxious little twerp and incredibly selfish." Go stand in the ULC and invite Jesus to come stand there with you and tell him what you are thinking about your brother. Then listen to his response. The odds are a million to one that he will say something kind and merciful about that little boy. Maybe he's going to suggest the boy admires you and so he wants to be by you. Maybe he's going to say the boy is bored and needs someone to play with. Or maybe he's going to say, "You know, I was sometimes really irritated by those apostles. They just wouldn't catch on to the message. I really had to dig deep to find patience. But it helped to remember that my Father loved them as much as He loved me. So I'd look at them with kindness and love."

You can run the Frame when you are frustrated with a teacher's style of teaching. You can use it if you get cut from soccer or you don't place in the dance competition. If you find yourself the victim of a horrible gossip circle, Jesus will be waiting for you. You can talk with him in the ULC about every thought, belief, or opinion you have. He will give you a perspective check and all the understanding, motivation, and support you need to PATH in even the toughest situations.

Do you see why they say that Christianity is revolutionary? **If you let your purpose (to know and love God) shape your thinking, then the way you work the rest of the Frame will lead you to be good to others in God's name.**

Consider a relationship that is challenging to you (a family member, classmate, teacher, coach). Focus on the individual.

- What do you think about this person?
- How do feel about this person?
- How do you act towards this person?
- What results are you getting from this relationship?

Pray the Sign of the Cross and ask Jesus to join you in the ULC.

Bring to mind the challenging relationship above.

Ask Jesus to help you want to think about it differently.

Using both your knowledge of Jesus and your imagination, identify a thought he might have about the person involved. Take your time. Try not to let your own thoughts bubble up to the surface.

Based on how you think Jesus might think about this person:

- How do you think about the relationship?
- How do you feel about it?
- Because of this how would you act?
- What results might you get?

Thank Jesus for helping you to reframe.

Close with the Sign of the Cross.

Chapter Seven

The Vehicle

I learned the basics of car mechanics from my dad.

TRUE TALES

When I was a kid, my family vacationed in Michigan. I looked forward to this week more than any other in the year. It was even better than Christmas. My anticipation would peak, though, when my dad began the preparations. Seeing Dad in the garage was the ultimate sign that Michigan was almost upon us.

The night before leaving he'd head out to the garage. Dad was a handyman, so he had tools for everything from car maintenance to house repair projects. Out would come the specially hung lights, including the awesome one on a retractable cord that could light up just about any corner or crevice of our station wagon. (My dad was very cool. Still is.)

And so, it would begin. He'd drain and replace the oil. Add blue water. Check the anti-freeze in the radiator. Tug on all the belts. Replace the windshield wipers. Clean out the air filter. Fill the tires. Then he'd crawl under the car and "have a look" just to make sure everything was shipshape.

These days most car owners leave these details to the professionals at Jiffy Lube. I think my dad even does. But he still knows what's what with how his cars run. Beyond general maintenance he knows the bigger picture of what makes them go.

There's a real lesson for all of us here. We're getting on the PATH in a particular vehicle and **we should have a bigger picture of what makes us go.**

The Big Myth

Right now your primary job, day in and day out, is to be a student. As with every worker, you will be happiest and feel most satisfied if you are finding value and success in your job. That means you need to find value and success in your school life.

I'll wait until the smirking subsides.

Still waiting.

All kidding aside, way too many students insist that what they learn in school isn't used in real life and, therefore, isn't of value for their future. On top of that, a great number report either having less success than they want in their studies or being successful because they aren't being challenged.

What's interesting is that these are all excellent examples of being LOST. School is *happening* to these folks. From their perspective, school is something Out There over which they have no control and **happiness is tough to come by when we have no sense of personal power or self-direction.**

If you're on the PATH, or wanting to get on the PATH, you need to debunk the Success Equation Myth which leads to this lack of personal power. Here's how the myth works.

You spend an awful lot of time during the school day tapping into your IQ, your Intelligence Quotient. Basically, this is your raw brain power and what people usually are referring to when they say, "He's smart" or "She's the smartest one in class." Tests in your various classes and annual state exams measure this kind of 'smart.' Folks that buy into the myth are working with a Success Equation that looks like this:

Success = IQ

If you've got the IQ, you can get the A's and you can be successful. The rest of us fall somewhere on a continuum of B's through F's. No wonder many folks don't feel they can be successful. They know where they fall on the IQ continuum.

The Truth of the Matter

This is a complete and total myth. The thought that your success and happiness in life is based on your IQ alone is complete nonsense. Quite the contrary, your VQ, or Virtue Quotient, is what plays the bigger role in experiencing success in any given situation or classroom. If you are on the PATH, you know this and so you've decided to do the Inside Job. You are working towards filling your suitcase with Virtues because you know that your VQ plays an enormous part in your Success Equation.

VQ = Prudence + Justice + Temperance + Fortitude

What exactly is the **Virtue Quotient?** It's the **compilation of the virtues you acquire.** It is a reservoir of inner skills (like honesty, perseverance, self-control and compassion) that sustains you from the inside out. Your VQ is a whole different way of being smart. The best news, especially for those of us who wish our IQ was a bit greater, is that **your VQ is yours to develop and improve.**

So here is the actual Success Equation:

Success = VQ x IQ

This equation is truly empowering. **Success in your faith life, in school, in relationships, and in your career is yours to manage by building your VQ.**

Let's work a few problems using our new equation.

> Example 1: Sally is bright (IQ = 8) and has her hand up all the time. She lacks friends because she is arrogant, boastful, and irritates people. Sally doesn't have many VQ people skills (VQ = 2). Her success total (2 x 8) is only 16 .
>
> Example 2: Meanwhile, behind Sally sits Andy who has average brainpower (IQ = 5). Andy never gets any A's and struggles to get B's and C's. He is dependable, trustworthy and brings out the best in others (VQ = 8). His success total (5 x 8) is 40.

8 x 2 = 16
IQ VQ

5 x 8 = 40
IQ VQ

Notice that Andy's success total is more than double that of Sally's. He's offsetting a lower IQ number by pumping up his VQ. Sally might be regarded as very successful academically, but Andy is the one I'd bet on for a lifetime of success. Not only will his growing virtues earn him respect and friendship during school, but they will translate to respect and healthy relationships in the future.

Things They Never Told You

Here's something else I learned from my dad: every car has two axles. An axle is a rod that connects two wheels together and allows them to rotate in unison. In most cars, the back axle gives stability and traction. The front axle does all the turning, directing, and powering up.

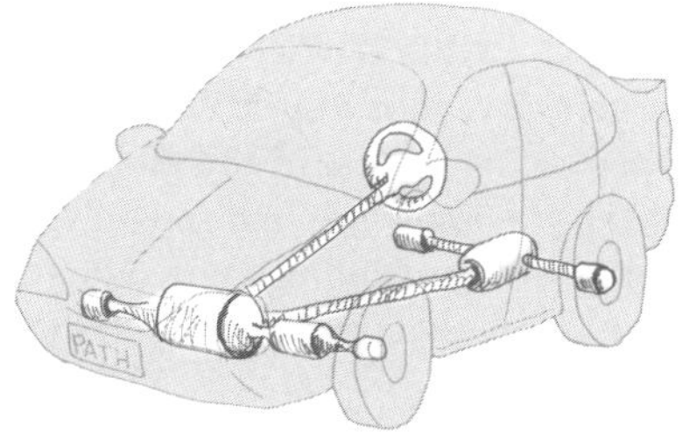

You can compare IQ and VQ to the front and back axle of the vehicle you take on your cross-country journey. Your IQ is the back axle, folks. It's important to the forward progress and balance of the vehicle, but it isn't running the show. That's the job of the front axle, or your VQ. It leads and aims the vehicle. It's your VQ that decides how you are going to handle a situation and how you are going to work through a problem. The VQ runs the show. Clearly, the front axle is more important than the back. Our examples prove it.

What about that all-important steering wheel and the steering column? Without them the car will still move, but it will not have a specific direction. A pothole will cause it to lose its bearings and a strong wind will slowly push it off course. That front axle needs to be connected to the steering column and the steering wheel for direction and correction from the driver.

Let's consider the steering column and wheel of your vehicle, the body you are traveling in for this lifelong journey. The steering wheel is God, and the steering column is the relationship you build through prayer, service, and study of God's ways. God is your source of direction and correction on the PATH.

We've established that God wants you to find complete happiness in this lifetime by coming to know and love Him. Notice that you and God hook together at the front axle, at your VQ rather than your IQ. It's time you exert some serious effort into figuring out how to make and keep that connection.

**You can raise your VQ.
Begin by pursuing a life-altering relationship with Jesus.
With him, you have the power
to keep your vehicle on the PATH.**

1. In which area of your VQ do you most want to improve? Prudence? Temperance? Justice? Fortitude?

2. How would you rate yourself on the IQ and VQ Scales (1-10)?

IQ Scale

Weak	1	2	3	4	5	6	7	8	9	10	Strong

VQ Scale

Weak	1	2	3	4	5	6	7	8	9	10	Strong

Pray the Sign of the Cross and ask Jesus to meet you in the ULC.

Offer an ACTS prayer about your VQ.

- Adore: Begin by praising God for this day and the opportunity to pray to Him.
- Confess: Apologize for anything you feel guilt or shame about.
- Thank: Thank God for always listening to, forgiving, and loving you.
- Supplicate: Ask God for strength and guidance in the area of your VQ where you want to grow.

End with the Sign of the Cross.

Chapter Eight

The Tipping Point

If you take just one lesson from the entire reading of the Bible it should be this: **God pursues you at all times.**

But how? There are no texts or emails from God. Yet this is how we are pursued these days. It's easy to find someone and to be found, right? Still, God chooses to pursue in ways that are neither obvious nor noisy. God's name has never been in your inbox. You won't find God retweeting Bible quotes, Instagramming or sending Snapchats. God's starting point is a complete 180° opposite of Social Media.

Like all pressing questions about God and faith, the answers can be found in the Bible. As it turns out, how God pursues us is not a great mystery. Check it out in Ezekiel 36:26-27.

I will give you a new heart,
and a new spirit I will put within you.
I will remove the heart of stone from your flesh
and give you a heart of flesh.
I will put my spirit within you.

Basically, Ezekiel is explaining some of what was going on during all that knitting and weaving in Psalm 139: God wove *His own Spirit* into your soul. **The most accessible source you have for finding God is within you.** Rather than reach you from the outside in, God pursues you from the inside. At all times, in all situations, and in every circumstance God can be found there.

Of course, God has other modes of contact. For instance, you can experience God through the tremendous diversity, beauty, and resilience of nature. A sunset, a flower pushing up through snow, and hurricane winds are God's Instagrams and Snapchats. The mercy, forgiveness, tenderness, and love you experience through family and friends allow God to reach out and physically minister to you. God touches, loves, and heals you through their hands.

These external examples of God are powerful and important. But they are also unpredictable and fleeting. The sun sets. That brave flower enjoys a short-lived spring. Hurt and resentment will rear their ugly heads again and even the strongest of your relationships will go through ups and downs.

It is this internal relationship you have with God that is constant and unfailing. No matter the changing circumstances of your situation and no matter your own dedication to the relationship, God will pursue you at all times. **Ultimately, your commitment to the Pursuit of All Things Holy will be as strong as your inner experience of God.**

Faith and the Frame

Thinking of yourself as loved and pursued tirelessly by God affects everything you feel, do, and get out of life.

When you are on the PATH, you stand in the ULC of the Frame *thinking* and *believing,* first and foremost, that you are not alone in the ULC. You begin the process of framing by getting in the yoke with God who is within, by your side at all times, equally invested in the outcome of every day, every choice and every relationship you have. This starting point makes all the difference. It enables you to be better than you could ever be in the ULC by yourself. Rather than walk alone, you choose to walk with God, seek guidance, and act on that guidance. When you do this, your true potential explodes exponentially. All it takes is a willingness on your part, a "Yes" offered by your free will.

$2 \times 2 = 2^2 = 4$

$2 \times 2 \times 2 = 2^3 = 8$

$2 \times 2 \times 2 \times 2 = 2^4 = 16$

$2 \times 2 \times 2 \times 2 \times 2 = 2^5 = 32$

$2 \times 2 \times 2 \times 2 \times 2 \times 2 = 2^6 = 64$

$2 \times 2 \times 2 \times 2 \times 2 \times 2 \times 2 = 2^7 = 128$

Critical Timing

As we've seen, you are at a critical stage of brain growth right now. The ultimate goal is for you to take personal responsibility for your future by harnessing the power of your brain. As your brain develops you are like the general contractor on a huge building project. You oversee all the decision making, negotiating, problem solving, and evaluating that goes into building a Grade A structure between your two ears.

As the creator of all life, God intends it to be this way. Wrapped into the process of your growing up is the opportunity for you to personally find God living within yourself and then choose to love Him, confident that yoked together you will reach your greatest potential and purpose. You **need** to become independent and to take the seat at the helm of your life. In fact, the world is in desperate need of young people who will shape themselves into future leaders and problem solvers and creative thinkers. Even more critical, the world is in desperate need of young people who master this transition while remaining deeply connected to God.

You have an important task to fulfill in God's name. You find that task and learn to complete it by living within God's will, and you learn God's will by building a steadfast friendship. Jesus made time to build that relationship—in the desert, in the garden, away from the city. Since he is our role model of what it means to be human, it follows that we need to do the same.

LEARNING THE FATHER'S WILL: JESUS AT PRAYER	
When He Prayed	**Where You'll Find It**
Before making a decision	Luke 6:12
On extended retreat	Luke 4:1-2
While preparing a meal	Mark 6:41
When afraid	Luke 22:41
For others to be strong and unified	John 17
To forgive people	Luke 23:46
Before meals	Mark 14:22
To help others pray	Matthew 6:5-13 and 14:22
To thank God	Matthew 11:25
At the end of a long day	Mark 6: 45-46

Building a Relationship

While obvious and otherworldly differences exist between you and God, building this friendship is not rocket science. You've already learned plenty of things about how to be a friend from your parents, teachers, siblings, and classmates. Jesus laid down some pretty solid ideas we can follow as well.

1. Learn about each other. I met my best friend in a bathroom. Seriously. We were seniors in high school. We were both guitar players, both singers, both pretty good at what we did musically. It made for quite a rivalry and a dislike based on absolutely nothing besides competitive spirits. One Friday afternoon during study hall we found ourselves awkwardly washing hands next to each other in the communal bathroom. It's hard to completely ignore another human being when she is the only other person inhabiting a space, so, begrudgingly I said, "Hey." She said, "Hey." Another awkward silence followed. I said, "What are you doing this weekend?" She told me. Turns out there was a massively cool open mic night at a nearby community college. She'd been going on Fridays. We talked a while about music genres, about our guitars, and, at some point, she invited me to go with her. I did. In the end, a couple simple questions over a hand washing broke down several years' worth of barriers and resulted in a longtime friendship. We opened a door to learning about each other and the friendship stuck.

Okay, we've got to admit that in the "learn about each other" department we are a bit behind since God knows everything about us. But it's never too late to start learning about God, just like it's never too late to break down barriers with a flesh and blood peer while in the bathroom. We have many, many sources of information to draw on as

So you're thinking about reading the Bible?

A few basics...

Build in success—Pick a regular time that you can make work.

Get away—Turn the sound off on your phone and close the cover of your computer. Close your door.

Use a Bible you can understand—the Catholic Youth Bible is a great choice.

Pray first—Just ask God to speak to you as you read. Then trust it will happen.

Bite-size is better than Super-size—It's a BIG book filled with great stuff. Don't worry about how long you read or how much you cover. Let God lead you to a cool phrase or interesting thought and then talk it over with Him.

It's not a novel—You don't need to begin on page one. Some good places to start: Mark's Gospel (shortest and easiest to understand), the Book of James, Psalms, Sirach, Wisdom, Paul's letters.

we strive to increase what we know about God. Reading the Bible is important, but *knowing how to read the Bible* is even more important. Lots of times we just read Scripture without understanding it, so we'll practice breaking that habit. Creation offers a boundless supply of information about God. Every animal, plant, landform, weather system, and atmospheric condition has something to teach us, if we take the time to learn. We have the lives of saints and holy folks, both famous and personal to us, to draw on. Listening to other people tell their faith stories introduces us to a whole new chapter about who God is and how God works.

2. Spend time. Duh. Think of the amount of time you spend on your best friends. There's the texting, the phone calls, times between and during classes, in the lunch room, at weekend parties, sports, gaming, and shopping. It's likely that your friend's mom knows all your favorite foods because you spend so much time at her house. Perhaps she refers to you as her adopted child. The point is, you hang out. A lot.

Spending time with God will challenge you to think outside the box of a human friendship, but not completely. Since God's creativity is endless, we should expect that God's ways of spending time with us in prayer will be equally creative. You can bring yourself into God's presence through silence, song, art, nature, meditation, group sharing, memories, imagination, visualization, exercise, and chores. Literally, praying can be done at all times and in many ways. As we explore them, pay attention to what works best for you and which situations respond to which prayer form.

3. Be honest. Honesty is a fundamental pillar of solid human relationships. We all want to be loved for being exactly who we are without having to hide any parts of ourselves for fear of rejection. Complete honesty is something we strive for in our closest relationships, but it can be tricky. Most of us have firsthand experience of falling short of this mark or being the casualty of someone else's dishonesty.

In fact, the ability to approach God with complete and total honesty is something of a breath of fresh air. **God will never turn away from the honest truth we offer.** God just wants us to share what we are thinking and feeling so that He can help us to see it through His eyes. By learning to speak honestly and listen well when in conversation with God, we open ourselves to receiving sacred guidance and wisdom. It's win-win for both of us.

4. Listen. Imagine that you are in a conversation. The person to whom you are speaking says something that immediately brings to mind a great come back or point you want to make. Rather than hearing the remainder of his story, you spend that time silently practicing what you are going to say once he is finished.

All of us are guilty of this. The challenge to listen presents itself in our friendship with God, too. The internal dialogue in our heads can be relentless, selfish, and pretty darn rude at times. It can feel beyond our control. But it isn't. We can learn strategies that will help us take control of these thought patterns, be more calm and less anxious, and, therefore, be more present to the people we are talking to and to God in prayer. The other side of this coin is that God 'speaks' differently than we are accustomed to hearing through our ears. Although it seems foreign to us, *God's language is merely under practiced.* The more you practice the better you get at translating. In other words, the better listener you become, the better a translator you will be.

5. Expect changes. Lifelong friends have endless stories to tell about each other and can reminisce about old times for hours. Some of those stories are funny, some involve life lessons learned together, and a few may recount experiences of broken hearts and tragedy. Stories become the backbone of a friendship and shape it over time. The person you were when you first met is not the person you are today or will be in the future. You're changed by knowing people. It's a fact of life.

Your friendship with God is similar, but with a twist. God will *invite* you to change over time. You'll feel it or hear it in your heart: a nudge to change the way you are treating someone, an idea that leads you to reach out to a classmate who seems to have few friends, a persistent feeling that you need to apologize for something. Who knows? Maybe you'll hear the whisper of a calling to a religious vocation. If you remain in a friendship with God, God will invite you to change.

Does God change, too? Nope. God is timeless and unchanging and needs no improving. But God's ability to reach you is limitless and that can sometimes catch us off guard. For instance, you may be growing comfortable in your way of praying and feel like you are in a groove connecting with God and then, all of a sudden, *poof!* God seems to be gone. Your prayer time turns into a torture festival and you are absolutely sure God has vacated the premises. More likely, though, God is trying to draw you closer by moving just outside of your field of vision so that you have to look a little deeper. God leads us closer to Him bit by bit because we can only understand in small pieces.

Looking Like God

In the opening scene of Walt Disney's *101 Dalmatians,* we see various dogs and their owners out on an afternoon walk through the neighborhood. While very funny to watch, the scene plays up the weird phenomenon that some humans seem to choose dogs that look like they do.

In a similar way, most of us know a married couple or two that seem to look alike. Scientists suggest that similar experiences (like lots of laughter or much anxiety) lead to similar facial wrinkles and physical habits (like slouching and holding your head up high). This might support the theory that married couples, in fact, can start to look more like each other over time.

What a great parallel to the loving friendship you can have with God!

- God lives within you and shares all your experiences.
- God will grow old with you.
- God will invite you to change and adapt in the years to come.

If you commit to this relationship and work at it every day, you can end up looking like the one you love. You can end up looking more and more like God.

God is a faithful and patient friend, completely devoted to you, and waiting for you within. But God allows you to define and determine the depth of your friendship and, therefore, the success of your PATH. It's up to you to choose to look like God.

Listed below are the five characteristics of friendship. Consider your friendship with Jesus and rank them from one through five. One is your area of strength and five needs the most work.

__ Learning about him through Scripture, conversations, and discussions with others.

__ Making time for him each day.

__ Speaking to him honestly about your thoughts, feelings, and behaviors.

__ Listening to him and trying to quiet your own thoughts.

__ Being willing to change things about yourself if you need to.

Pray the Sign of the Cross and then ask Jesus to come and be with you.

Think about this quote: "We have to pray with our eyes on God, not on the difficulties."

Write down the names of three people in whom you see qualities of Jesus.

List three things in nature that teach you something about God.

Recall two times you have felt God's presence in a powerful way. Jot them down using a one-word descriptor for each.

Now close your eyes and thank God for being present to you in all these ways. Then sit for a couple moments and listen.

Close with the Sign of the Cross.

Chapter Nine

Shifting Planks

Blessed are your eyes, because they see.
Matthew 13:16

Remember that girl I met in the bathroom? She became my closest confidant. Until that chance interaction, we had an intense dislike for each other. I had decided that she was conceited, a showoff, cocky, and proud about her skills. Had I based this charming evaluation on personal interactions with her, concrete evidence, interviews, or facts? None of the above. My evaluation and opinion of her were built on my own gut reactions to what I thought about her. I saw her as a threat and way too competent in the same areas in which I was competent. She was someone I had to be better than.

Although this is a crazily unattractive picture of myself, it is all true. Happily, I can report that my thoughts were debunked and replaced by a deep respect for her abilities and friendship, as well as for the music we ended up making together. But I didn't learn to unpack this story and all its deeper meanings until I starting down the PATH.

Basically, the Tale of the Toilet (couldn't resist!) teaches us the importance of clarity in the Upper Left Corner of the Frame. If our initial thoughts are out of whack or erroneous, the actions we take and the resulting outcomes we experience will be equally whacky and erroneous.

So, how do we check our thinking to make sure it is spot-on and, therefore, trustworthy?

Before going further, let's do an experiment. Read the following sentence carefully.

FINISHED FILES ARE THE RESULT OF YEARS OF SCIENTIFIC STUDY COMBINED WITH THE EXPERIENCE OF MANY YEARS.

Now read it again.

All right, go back and count all the letter F's you see in the sentence.

What number did you get? Write it here: _______.

Most people see three F's in the sentence. They see them in the important words that carry the content of the sentence: finished, files, scientific. A smaller number see four or five and typically only 20% see all six. Three F's are in the word 'of'. Our eyes tend to pass over these because they aren't important to understanding the content. If you didn't see six F's you likely missed some in the word 'of'.

Perspective As Plank

What can we learn from this experiment? It was straightforward and no attempt was made to trick you. Just count some letters that all look the same. The fact that 80% of folks tend to miss some of those letters begs a much bigger question. *If we can't see correctly in concrete and simple situations, why do we assume that we can see clearly in complicated situations?* Why did I decide all those spiteful things about a fellow classmate I'd barely spoken with when I can't even count F's correctly? Why? Because **we think we see things the way they are.** To which Jesus said:

Why do you notice the splinter in your brother's eye,
but do not perceive the plank in your own eye?
You hypocrite! Remove the plank from your eye first,
then you will see clearly to remove the splinter from your brother's eye.
Matthew 7:3,5

Count on Jesus to tell it like it is. I had one enormous plank blocking my vision when I looked at this girl. That plank was my pride.

What we are talking about here are our thinking habits. How we think about things gives rise to our perspective—the way we see situations, the way we see other people, and even the way we see ourselves.

Everyone reading this has a set of thinking habits. These habits form your perspective. Two simple examples of this are the optimist and the pessimist. An optimist's patterns of thinking lead her to feel hopeful and positive about the future. A pessimist's thinking patterns lead her to expect the worst.

Because of these thinking patterns, a family vacation to Disney in the minivan will find our optimist and pessimist with entirely different opinions about the upcoming vacation.

If our thinking habits are faulty or off kilter, we will reap the logical results of our skewed thoughts. The disgruntled young man in the backseat is setting himself up for a pretty hateful vacation, even though his younger brother will return home with nothing but awesome memories. Prideful thoughts formed my perspective of my classmate, so I saw her as a nemesis. That's what she remained until my thinking pattern was shifted by a simple and unexpected conversation in a bathroom. Everything changed on that shift: I saw her differently, I felt differently about her so I acted differently, and I gained a true friend.

The shift in my perspective caused me to see myself more clearly, too. By removing my own plank, I was able to begin addressing a real temptation: pride.

A faulty thinking habit can rear its ugly head in any situation. Many students bring sabotaging thinking habits into a classroom. If you approach a class thinking "I'm stupid" or "When am I ever going to need to know this in real life," you set yourself up for a miserable experience. What you think drives the experience in that class. It affects how you feel, what you do and what you get. It's the Frame in action.

"I was looking at life through binoculars, but I was holding them the wrong way. Learning about 'seeing' helped me turn them around."
-Charlie

Not all faulty thinking habits are as negative as mine were in the infamous bathroom example or as sabotaging classroom thoughts. Sometimes a pattern is no longer effective because the situation has changed, but we haven't realized we need to modify our thinking pattern. For example, parents have to learn new perspectives in parenting as their kids grow older. They move from protector to supporter to sounding board to sage as their children's needs change. This can be a struggle for some parents. Remember, parents are plank-prone, too.

We can take great comfort and find much hope in knowing that the forebearers of our faith also struggled in the plank department.

Peter: The plank in Peter's eye seriously raised Jesus's rile and led to one of the few times in Scripture when Jesus exhibited anger. Jesus was foretelling the suffering he would have to forgo (Matthew 16) and Peter refused to believe it. In fact, Peter adamantly disagreed with Jesus. In response, Jesus actually told him to "Get behind me, Satan." Ouch! Obviously, Peter still had a ways to go before *seeing clearly* what Jesus was teaching!

Philip: Jesus and the disciples were having one of their private teaching lessons (John 14:1-14) when Jesus said, "If you know me, then you know my Father." To which Philip said, "Master, show us the Father, and that will be enough for us." Can't you just see Jesus slapping his own forehead in frustration and wanting to say, "Duh!!" in a pretty sarcastic tone? All this time he is *God with them* and trying to get that across to these future leaders of the Church. Here's Philip saying aloud what they are all thinking: "I don't get it." PLANK!

Mary Magdalene and the Apostles: After Jesus rose from the dead, neither Mary Magdalene (John 20:14-15), the disciples on the road to Emmaus (Luke 24:16), nor Peter, Thomas or Zebedee out fishing (John 21:4) recognized Jesus when he appeared to them, even though they had spent three years following him and learning from him.

Saul: In the earliest days of the Church, Saul devoted all his energies to hunting down and annihilating Christians. The plank in Saul's eye was so big that he had to be thrown from his horse and blinded for three days in order to remove it. (Acts 9:1-19) God even changed his name to Paul. From then on Paul saw with completely new eyes and perspective. When he went from Saul to Paul, his Frame changed.

Planks are simply a part of being human. We have to expect them, look for them, and work to remove them.

If You Are on the PATH, You Are on Plank Alert

This plank business is serious stuff. Thinking clearly and seeing rightly is a lifelong mission for a Christian, as the disciple stories above show. How are we to correctly figure out what God has in mind for us if our pride, anger, anxiety, or a myriad of other wooden beams are jutting out of our eyeballs? (Okay, it's not literal, but it's a cool visual.)

It's likely that we can all see the importance of 'de-planking' ourselves for the good of our relationships with other people. No one wants their family dinner to be as uncomfortable as having their braces tightened. Nor do we enjoy being in the middle of a big fight with a group of friends. Ultimately, we all desire a strong family life and a supportive network of friends. De-planking is a reliable tool for helping us to build those solid bonds.

I would submit, however, that there is an even more pressing reason for pursuing a plank-free life. It's one of those higher thoughts in faith that you need to start wrestling with now that you are at The Big Shift and preparing to PATH for a lifetime. It flows directly from what we know True Happiness to be. Remember, this is *True Happiness,* not cheap, of-this-world-fleeting-changing-unreliable happiness.

Pay attention now. This is important!

As Catholics, we believe that God loved us into life. Without God's grace and energy we would simply not exist. Period. (Somehow contemporary humans can forget this, so caught up are we in all our coolness and inventions. But I digress.) Flowing from the *amazing* reality that God gave us life is our desire to say at the top of our lungs, "Hey, thanks!" We do this by developing the gifts, talents, and desires God gave us. When we become what God envisions us to be, then, and only then, do we find true happiness.

Which begs the question: How could we possibly ever hope to become what God envisions us to be if we have planks in our eyes that keep us from seeing what is actually going on in our relationships and circumstances? This is the most pressing reason for seeking to live a plank-free life. I want to do my best for God. I want to be all that God imagines for me. Take away anything that clouds my vision or distorts my view. Break all the Funhouse Mirrors if you have to! Let me see clearly so that I can share God's vantage point and know how I can do His will.

We de-plank in order to attend to our first order of business. We de-plank so we can turn to God and say, "Here I am. You made me for this world and I come to do your will in it. Show me how and help me to see it."

The Necessary First Step

When you undertake the task of identifying and then removing a plank, what you are actually doing is improving your understanding of a situation by altering the way you think about that situation. **A change in perspective takes place when you change what you are thinking.**

How do you go about changing what you think? Many tools can help you find a new perspective, but they all require the same first step: **Fess Up.**

Assume and admit that there is stuff you don't know. You do not possess 20/20 vision into the motives and meanings behind other people's behavior. It's a simple concept: you live in your own brain and it's tough enough learning how to control the thoughts and emotions it generates. It's not possible to establish such insight into or control over others.

When you find yourself in a relationship or situation that is difficult, challenging, or rubbing you the wrong way, you should immediately fall back on the mantra: "I am blind. I am blind. I am blind." You are not seeing something clearly in the situation. Even if you are on the right track with your thinking, you are not all the way there. Admit it to yourself. Recognize your limitations.

How might 'fessing up' look in real life?

- Your best friend just gave you a weird look in the hallway. Rather than deciding she is angry at you or interpreting the look *at all,* ask yourself first, "What am I not seeing?"
- Your coach takes you out of the game at a crucial moment. Challenge yourself to *question what you don't know* about how he reached that decision.

In both of these examples you are respecting the fact that **you are blind** and that you don't see anything exactly as it is.

The Rest of the Story

Once you've admitted you are blind, it's time to start looking for ways to correct your vision. You have several options that vary in their degree of consequences:

1. Create a Crisis. Crises are very effective in uprooting planks and re-orienting thinking patterns. For instance, the Civil War was a national crisis. In the end the faulty belief that human beings could be used as slaves was corrected. That grotesque plank was removed. However, the cost of that crisis in lives, pain, and fallout was extraordinary: over 600,000 deaths and decades of rebuilding and bitter resentment.

Yes, you could create a crisis within your group of friends or between you and your parents. But is the aftermath really a price you are willing to pay and inflict when there are other strategies at your disposal? While crises may get us to see things differently, several less painful and more loving strategies can bring about a clearer, plank-free perspective.

2. Be Direct. This is the most effective and mature strategy, but also the most challenging. Tackle your blindness head on by going directly to the individual. Explain what you see happening. Admit that you are likely not seeing the whole picture and ask if you can talk it through and come to a new understanding. For this route to be successful, participants need to communicate effectively as both speakers and listeners. We'll work on some of those skills in the chapters ahead to give you confidence in this strategy.

TRUE TALES

After casting a musical for my sixth graders, a parent of a wonderfully talented young lady came to me to talk about how disappointed her daughter was with the role she received. It wasn't one of the biggest parts in the play. The student was thinking that I didn't like her voice or that I perhaps had some sort of grudge against her. I was stupefied! I explained to the mom and later to the student that the role I gave her, though smaller than some, was the most demanding role in the play. I had put my best voiced actress in it, thrilled to know she would completely rock that scene! All of us—student, mom, and teacher—benefitted by learning about what we weren't seeing.

3. Ask Others How They See It. Who will see a situation differently than you? Anyone. Since no two people see through the same eyeballs, you'll be able to expand your sight by talking to others. One important caveat: it is best to ask the insights of those you respect and admire, not those who will happily agree with you in order to please you. Sometimes a best friend is *not* the voice you should listen to. He's likely your friend because you share the same opinions and perspectives. His voice may only serve to increase the size of your plank. Consider a classmate you respect, an older sibling or a trusted teacher, your parent or confirmation sponsor. Who can give you a wider view than the one you have right now?

4. Swap out Your Role. This strategy asks you to use your powers of imagination. Instead of looking at this situation from your own shoes, try to see it from someone else's. Imagine you are the school counselor or your parent. How does it look from that vantage point? How would your older sister describe what's going on? How does the other team's coach see that substitution? What would your grandma be seeing? Each of these jiggles the plank by asking you to step outside of your regular vantage point and try to see from another angle.

5. Talk to Yourself in Questions Only. In your head or on a piece of paper begin a dialogue about this event between your Blind Self and your Seeing Self. Your Seeing Self gets to play the role of God. It might sound something like this:

Blind: What did she look at me like that for?
Seeing: You saw that, too? Where do you think she was coming from?
Blind: What does that have to do with anything?
Seeing: Well, could something have happened in her last class that we don't know about?
Blind: How am I supposed to know?
Seeing: Did you think of asking her?
Blind: Why are you always so smart?

Or, it could go like this:

Talking to yourself in questions asks you to do just that: question yourself. Eventually the conversation will lead you to an outline of your plank sitting right there in your eye (or heart). It will help you to see it clearly and start rooting it out.

And What about Jesus?

Since he is your role model for everything human, you should pay some serious close attention to what Jesus did in this regard. He didn't have magic powers that allowed him to read people's minds or have clarity of thought without any effort. That's one of the greatest Excuse Shield tricks in the marginal believer's arsenal: "Yeah, he was human, but in a different kind of way." Back to the Catechism where it is written:

> "The Son of God worked with human hands; he thought with a human mind. He acted with a human will, and with a human heart he loved. Born of the Virgin Mary, he has truly been made one of us."
>
> (Catholic Church, 470)

Jesus had the same raw materials to work with that you have at your disposal: intellect, emotion, free will, flesh, and blood. Ultimately, *he chose* to 'live humanly' the way God intended humans to live. He hit the reboot button and showed you how to undo all that was broken when Adam and Eve took that apple from the serpent. Basically they said to God: "You know, we've got a better idea. We're going to try this human thing our way." Jesus showed you how to rewrite their answer, turn yourself back to the PATH and say: "You made me to reflect your goodness. I trust your plan for me. Show me what you want and I will do it."

If you are paying attention, you realize that Jesus's whole purpose was to help you and me be plank-free. His human life was about helping people return their focus to God and to their divine destiny in relationship with Him. Jesus did this by exposing the planks that blocked them from seeing things as God sees and, wisely, he used unique and relevant strategies that captured their attention and broke through the 'same old same old.' For example:

- He challenged hypocrites.
- His parables included fantastic and unexpected plot twists.
- He knew his audience and used the stuff of their daily lives in his stories and lessons—nets, storms at sea, gardening, parenting, and cleaning.
- He got his hands dirty and healed people with mud and spit and touch.

- He hung out with poor people, outcasts, sinners, and those the cool group avoided.
- He led by listening, healing, challenging, and sacrificing and crowds followed.

Jesus used every trick in the book to help identify and eradicate planks and blindness—he was direct, he questioned, he offered his own example as a gauge for measuring our efforts, and he turned familiar tales topsy-turvy to grab folks off guard so they could see from a different point of view.

LOST vs PATH	
PLANKED!!	**DE-PLANKING!**
I am blind.	I am blind.
I don't know I'm blind, so I think I see everything clearly.	I know I'm blind and realize I may not see a situation clearly.
Therefore I believe I am right. I sink in my heels.	I go to the Upper Left Corner and ask Jesus to join me there.
In tough situations I blame others for my problems or make excuses for my failings.	By looking at a tough situation with his guidance, I am able to gain a new perspective.
I give all my power away and am miserable. I continue to be LOST.	Plank is moved and I see more clearly. I keep to the PATH.

Cross. Resurrection. What?

If the disciples were reading this chapter with you, they might even suggest that Jesus created a crisis to help them see clearly. Looking backwards through the prism of the cross and resurrection, all his other plank-defying strategies began to make sense to those first believers.

Initially, it seemed that Jesus's three years of ministry came to an abrupt and disastrous end at his trial and crucifixion. During the three days Jesus was in the tomb, the disciples hid in fear, dreams destroyed, trying to make sense of what had happened. They had turned their lives upside down to follow him and thought they were on to something good. They thought they were beginning to see clearly. But then he was crucified and all his selflessness and goodness seemed pointless.

Yet, there he was before them, alive again. What did it mean? What became clear to them when they realized that he had risen from the dead? What plank did the resurrection finally loosen for them? Paul tells us in 1 Corinthians 15:14:

> *If Christ has not been raised,*
> *then empty too is our preaching;*
> *empty, too, your faith.*

For the disciples, Jesus resurrection is the 'Aha moment' that put all the pieces of a three-year puzzle in place. Before the resurrection, they had glimpses of what Jesus was saying. They got it sometimes. For example, when Jesus asked Peter, "Who do you say that I am?" Peter responded, "You are the Christ, the Son of the living God." (Matthew 16:16) That clarity had evaporated before the end of the chapter, however, when Jesus overheard the disciples arguing about which of them was the greatest in the group. They completely missed the point that *great means least.* The plank in action.

The resurrection became the cement that solidified all their 'almost-get-it' moments into enduring, unshakable faith. It confirmed all of Jesus's works and teachings. He *conquered death.* Who could possibly do that but one with divine authority and power over all things? *He really was God* who came to earth to show us the way back to Him after the catastrophic apple incident by Adam and Eve. All the healings and stories, the miracles and the forgiveness, the way he approached everyone with mercy and love and compassion, that was all really God *showing us just what is possible inside a human body,* if we choose to yoke ourselves up with Jesus and find our strength and purpose in him.

That was the new perspective the disciples gained through the Resurrection of Jesus. The final plank was removed and in the future they stood in the ULC of the Frame with a whole new way of thinking and a whole new perspective.

It changed everything. The Big Shift had happened.

1. Identify a part of your life about which you are dissatisfied (examples: a class, a relationship, a personal weakness).

2. How do you think about yourself and the other people involved in this situation?

3. Look at the list below and circle the de-planking approaches with which you are most comfortable. Underline any you would find difficult to use.

Put a check next to those you will try regarding the situation in question #1.

- Be direct.
- Ask others how they see it.
- Swap out your role.
- Talk to yourself in questions only.
- Create a crisis.

Pray the Sign of the Cross and then ask Jesus to come and be with you.

In the center of a piece of paper, put an initial identifying the situation in #1 above.

Beneath the initial put a de-planking approach you are willing to try.

Under this write 'JC and Me.'

Out loud ask Jesus to help you with the next step.

Use the rest of the page to brainstorm ways to put the approach into practice. You can write in sentences or bullets, use code, draw or a combination of these.

When you are finished, thank Jesus for always being in the yoke with you.

Close with the Sign of the Cross.

Chapter Ten

Your Ancestry: The Fall

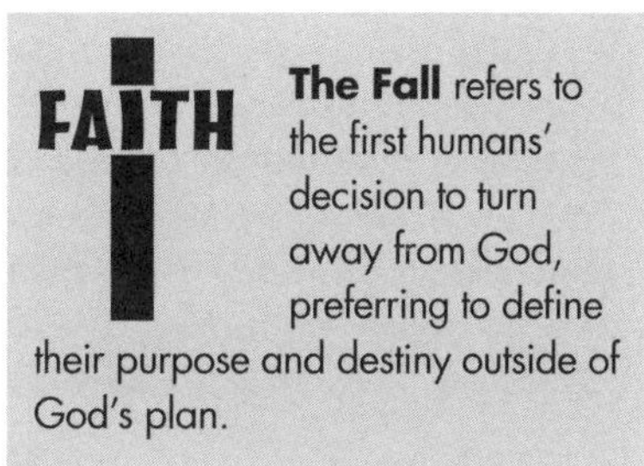

We toss the word 'sin' around a lot without ever getting to the core of what we mean by it. Yes, sin means doing something wrong, maybe even evil. Yes, it likely means that we've broken a commandment. Yes, often we get in trouble when we sin because we get caught. Yes, sins need to be confessed to be absolved and we need to make amends with those we've hurt.

But none of this really gets to the core of the problem. Where did sin come from, anyway? Why am I stuck with it? How can I get rid of it? And, seriously……????? What happened in the Garden of Eden? Like, for real?

Let's start by clearing up a simple point. You're old enough for this now. The Church teaches that the story of Adam and Eve uses "figurative language" (Catholic Church, 390) to explain a fundamental event that took place at the beginning of human history. Figurative means symbolic. We don't actually have records of an Adam and Eve and we can't point to a Garden of Eden on a map. Rather, God inspired the writer of Genesis with this fantastic story that explains all the ins and outs of:

- how humans were created in Original Holiness and
- how they ended up choosing the opposite of that intended purpose.

The rest of the Bible recounts the story of humans trying to figure out the way back to the Garden and Original Holiness.

Adam and Eve — **Noah** — **Abraham** — **Isaac** — **Jacob**

What is this Original Holiness and what would it have been like to live within it? The Catechism can help us with this. According to it, the first human was "not only created good, but also established in friendship with God" and enjoyed "harmony with himself and with the creation around him." (Catholic Church, 374)

Remember how we had an entire chapter on how important it is to establish a close friendship with God, how God lives within you and patiently waits for you to start working on that friendship, and how the more time you spend with God the more you start to 'look' like and reflect God's image. Pre-fall humans didn't need chapters like that. They were doing it. Their friendships were intact and they had a perfect pipeline to God. They knew God and they knew themselves, living plank-free. They were filled with contentment and joy, knowing that they were created by and united with God, enjoying holiness because they lived true to God and true to their nature. Their nature was to find their meaning in God, and they were doing so. That is **Original Holiness.** They PATHed their way to fulfillment.

It is doubtful that the word *I* was a part of their vocabulary. *We* was the pronoun of choice.

Evil Is Real

How could it all have gone so wrong? If these earliest humans were so exquisitely happy, what could ever have enticed them away?

Our faith teaches us that God fashioned all the cosmos out of an amazing gush of love and creativity. Because God loves creation perfectly, it is God's desire that we freely love Him back. Even we know that forcing someone to love us isn't possible—it's pathetic and a power play. Because God desires to be chosen, God allows the possibility of being rejected.

We all know the story of the serpent in the Garden of Eden. This slimy slitherer represents the **fallen angels,** creatures who "radically and irrevocably rejected God." (Catholic Church, 392)

Not only did these fallen angels radically and irrevocably reject God, it was and remains their mission to entice others to do the same. So the serpent (representing the fallen angels), knowing humans' weaknesses, said the fateful words about the apple: "God knows well that the moment you eat of it your eyes will be opened and you will be like gods." (Genesis 3:5) The Evil One, through the mouth of the serpent, cunningly introduced us to a new concept. His suggestion that we will be like gods carries a really powerful, nature-shifting evil with it: he suggests that we try living apart from God, separate and distinct. **He wants us to live like God, but not in God any longer.** The first humans enjoyed original holiness because they wholeheartedly embraced their intended nature in God; the serpent tempted them to shift their focus from "all eyes on God" to "all eyes on me."

In those bites of apple, free will chose itself over God. *That* is The Fall. **Humans chose to live outside their nature by living apart from God.** *This is the heart of evil.*

The Old Testament is the wild and detailed story of many generations struggling with the reality of this really tremendous downfall (see timeline below). Humans found themselves struggling with famine, hatred, floods, slavery, and disease. The whole balance of nature had truly been thrown off because the crowns of creation (human beings) abandoned their role as guardian by abandoning their nature *in God.* We were meant to have mastery over the world, yet were unable to master our own selves. (Catholic Church, 377) Everything was in a tailspin.

God immediately started reaching out to the human family by raising righteous men and women to live and lead by example. Prophet after prophet spoke God's words, intending to lead the people back to Him. They foretold of a messiah who would come to save them and suffer on their behalf. The

Isaiah **Daniel** **Esther**

people experienced times of great difficulty and times of great hope. But what the Old Testament account of history confirms is pretty obvious: **we were going to take the long way home as a result of the desire to live for self.**

I'm feeling pretty much like a Debbie Downer, but there's no way to really spin this whole discussion of the Fall without facing the facts. Might as well admit it and call a spade a spade. There's some real gunk to deal with in the human soul. Each of us, in the private corners of our own hearts and in the courtroom of our own conscience, can look at this sad story and say: "Yeah, it's true. I know what good really is and I often miss the mark. A lot of the reason is that I focus on myself and what makes me happy, not necessarily what God is drawing me to."

The New Adam

So there we were, a human race completely planked. Our map back to the Garden was smudged all over by sin and weakness and we were blinded by our own will. Still, the Old Testament reminds us that generations of wanderers struggled to turn back to God by grateful obedience to His will. God patiently worked with them, meeting them where they were on the journey, and helping them master themselves ever so gradually. But what the human race really needed was a *breakthrough.*

In the fullness of time, God did breakthrough with Jesus. The Church uses the title of 'The New Adam' to stress the importance of this breakthrough. So, what does it mean? Basically, everything our first parents did wrong, Jesus did right. Where they gave in to temptation, he stayed strong.

FAITH

What's all this 'fullness of time' stuff? Imagine a glass of water slowly filling up. Eventually the glass is full. In faith-talk the fullness of time refers to the coming of Jesus into the world. God had been preparing us for this coming so as to increase our ability to see him in a human form. Signs and prophecies had been handed down from age to age. A race of people was striving to be true to God. They knew God was going to come because they had heard it foretold. **The fullness of time refers to when God determined that all was prepared for this coming—the cup was full—and God entered the world in flesh and blood.**

Where they were proud, he was humble. Where they were self-involved, he was God-focused. **He's the New Adam, the one who does 'human' correctly.**

It was the most unexpected and earth-shattering event of all time: a baby was born and he was God. This may be the coolest yet most elusive truth of our faith: Jesus is God. Sure we say this and we confess it in the Creed every Sunday, but do we ever stop and just *think about what that really means?*

- *Jesus* has been for all time and will remain for all time.
- *Jesus* created the cosmos.
- *Jesus* is abhorred by the Evil One.
- *Jesus* endured the gut-wrenching choice by the first humans to turn away from him.
- *Jesus* sent those prophets and patriarchs to try to lead us back.

Ultimately, in a mind-blowing display of devotion and humility, "*Jesus* came down from heaven and became man."

But why?

To help us see. He showed us *what it looks like* to know and love God completely and fiercely. He showed us *what it looks like* to be good to others and to serve them in the name of God. He showed us *what it looks like* to keep our eyes off of self and on the truth about who we are in God's presence. He showed us *what it looks like* to stare down and defeat the Evil One.

Jesus, our God, longs for us to return to him. He desires our company and our union. Talk about the Mystery of Faith! How could a being so supreme and so beyond our comprehension love us so completely as to pine and court us for thousands of years? This is the most perfect Lover any of us will ever know. Completely faithful. Completely devoted. Determined to win us back.

For those who are LOST, the story of Jesus leaves them scratching their heads. "What was the big deal? What's all the fuss about? He was a nice guy who died a tragic death. Rumor has it he came back to life. Whatever."

But for those on the PATH, Jesus provided a concrete road map home. By becoming human, God got down and dirty, literally got skin in the game

with us. Jesus said, "Come after me." (Mk 1:17) He intends to lead us to the Garden, back to where we belong. Our eyes are clear again and we have a PATH to follow.

Jesus was strong against temptations, humble, and God-focused.

1. Against what temptations do you need to be strong?

2. In what areas are you humble?

3. When are you most able to remain God-focused and on the PATH?

Pray the Sign of the Cross and then ask Jesus to come and be with you.

Write a prayer to Jesus about being on the PATH with him on the way back to Original Holiness. *Do not use the words I, me, or my. Instead use words like us, ours and we.* Focus your prayer on *being with Jesus* on the PATH, rather than on a solo journey.

When your prayer is completed, close with the Sign of the Cross.

Chapter Eleven

The Evil Emperor

From World Wars to family fights, from power hungry despots to vengeful classmates, the draw to be all about ourselves is destructive and universal. We can see and feel its effects on the world's stage and in our own private lives.

Now that we have covered the basics about being on the PATH versus being LOST and have a pretty good handle on the Law of 90/10, the Frame, and Planks, it's time to start plotting a course for effectively dealing with the evil around us. First we'll spend some important time learning how it works. It's just plain smart to know what you're up against. Then we'll turn to what we can do about it, both in the moment and after the fact.

"If I've already thought through a situation and have a response prepared ahead of time, in the event temptation rears its ugly head, it is that much easier to resist."
–Tim Teboe

Before beginning we need a working language. How we refer to the presence and reality of evil is something of a matter of preference: a conniving snake, fallen angels, the prince of this world, the Devil, complete with red horns and a pitchfork. For the purposes of this book, I'm going to refer to this **malicious reality of evil** as the **Evil Emperor** or EE for short. It fits the theme of an extended and demanding Quest for Good, which is an excellent definition of the PATH. (And yes, I am a fan of *The Lord of the Rings* and *Star Wars.*)

The Evil Emperor is after your soul because he has "irrevocably rejected God" (Catholic Church, 392) and is determined to stymie God's Grand Design by conquering the crown of creation—us humans. His primary area of expertise is incredibly effective: he messes with your thoughts and implants planks. He works *inside your brain.* **It is absolutely crucial that you take control of the Big Shift that is occurring in there right now. If you do not the Evil Emperor certainly will.**

You would think that we would see this happening and be able to stop it. Why is it so hard to recognize and combat temptation? Because the EE excels in two particular areas:

1. **The Emperor knows your weakness.** Pride? Self-doubt? Laziness? Procrastination? He knows where you are most vulnerable and pushes that button. It's the easiest way to get a foothold into your soul. Then he weasels in further. I've mentioned I have an issue with pride. When I look back, I can see the EE really started working on me there when I was in high school.

> "Watch and pray that you may not enter into temptation. The spirit indeed is willing, but the flesh is weak."
> –Jesus, Matthew 26:41

2. **The Emperor makes evil look attractive.** He is a master of disguise. He knows how to dress temptations up in appealing wrapping paper. That apple in the Garden looked red and juicy, not a bruise to be seen. It showed no outward signs of disaster or doom. It looked good!! Just so, accusing that classmate of being conceited allowed me to ignore the fact that I was full of pride, and it certainly kept me from being good to others in God's name. Chalk one up for the EE.

> "The devil comes as everything you ever wished for."
> –Tucker Max

You've learned that your thoughts give rise to your feelings and your actions. Think about yourself. What is a negative or unkind thought that you harbor? For example,

- "I'm stupid at math."
- "My parents like my brother better than me."
- "That girl is so conceited."

Identify a negative or unkind thought that sometimes shows up in your head. Locate one now.

Waiting.

That thought is an example of where you must do battle with the Emperor. In the ULC, you can either ignore the EE's presence or acknowledge it. If you ignore it, you will be unknowingly manipulated by him. If you acknowledge it and turn to Jesus for strength, he will help you de-plank and create a new way of thinking in that situation.

> "Get behind me, Satan!"
> – Matthew 16:23

You can let yourself be a pawn in the Emperor's game (that would be LOST) or you can choose to be a child of light, one of the redeemed, a sheep of the flock and on the PATH. The better you get at recognizing invasive, negative-maybe-even-sinful thoughts within yourself and the sooner you interrupt them, the more effective a defense you can put up against the EE's advances.

1. Privately consider the sin you find yourself most often committing and needing to confess during the Sacrament of Reconciliation.

2. Pinpoint a few specific examples of when the Emperor used that sin to lead you off the PATH.

Begin with the Sign of the Cross.

Close your eyes and visualize the Frame.

Focus on the ULC and ask Jesus to be with you there to help guide your thinking.

Now tell him about the struggle you have with this sin. Share the thoughts you have regarding the power it seems to have over you.

Next, ask him to help you be courageous when the Emperor tempts you with it.

Listen quietly for a bit. What new PATH-like thoughts come to mind for you? That's Jesus responding.

Trust he is with you and enjoy his presence.

Close with the Sign of the Cross.

CHAPTER TWELVE

Habits of Grace

Let's get something out in the open right away. We all have **Negative Thinking Habits (NTHs),** attitudes or ways of thinking that block our ability to see a situation or person correctly. These are our personal planks and no one likes to admit or talk about them. Spending time lamenting the unwanted things we wish were not a part of us doesn't make our Top 10 Favorites List either. To top it off, we tend to see our bad habits as too hard to change and our shortcomings not as serious as someone else's.

With thoughts like these we are already playing into the EE's game plan. If we aren't willing to look at the habits and thoughts that hold us back from the PATH, then he's won already. **What we need is a shift in perspective.**

Grace Like Rain

We know that our thinking is the captain of our ship; where it steers we go. We know that the Frame is the super power of the Inside Job. This means we can use the Frame to think about our Negative Thinking Habits in a new way and, thereby, chart a new course. We're going to stand in the ULC and look at our NTHs and rename them as *opportunities.*

Heads up. We're going to go deep again.

How, you ask, can something like pride, envy, or whining ever be an opportunity? When you are God and understand the ins and outs of how the creature has fallen, you get pretty creative in your attempts to help them back home. Loving each of us despite our weaknesses and witnessing our struggles with evil and temptation, God reaches out to us by saturating all of creation with Grace. **Every corner of our world is saturated with God's presence, anticipating our return and making that return possible, even at our broken**

and weakest places. This is Grace. Like a rain shower that fills every space of invisible atmosphere or the canvas that is the background of an artist's painting, God's grace is all around us.

Grace is God's complete commitment to be with you on the PATH. It is the perpetual gift of God's presence in your life, supporting, protecting, and sustaining you on your way back to Him. No expiration date. Ever.

Let's be clear: we did nothing to earn this gift. Grace is given to us by God. But, we have to do something to benefit from this gift. **We have to notice it. We have to respond to it. We have to work with it.**

Our Free Will is always respected by God. Unlike the EE who will infiltrate our minds while we aren't looking and manipulate our thinking while we are unaware, God is a gentleman who waits patiently for us to walk through the door He has opened for us. He waits for us to notice and choose Him. It's like our own chance to undo what Adam did. Rather than grab that apple, we double-down and look to God's grace for strength. When we do, transformation happens. We are changed for the better.

Need proof?

The bleeding woman—A woman living near the Sea of Galilee had been hemorrhaging for 12 years. She was dirt poor after spending all her money on doctors who had only made her illness worse. One day, Jesus passed through her town. She had heard of this man, and in a leap of faith she reached out to him, believing if she could even touch the hem of his cloak that would be plenty. Sure enough, she was healed. Normal day: Grace became visible; she responded; she was changed. (Mark 5:25-29)

Lydia—While praying on the Sabbath by the river in Philippi, Lydia, a freed slave and working woman, heard Paul preaching about Jesus. She listened closely and was deeply touched by his message. On an impulse she asked to be baptized. Normal day: Grace became visible; she responded; she was changed. (Acts 16:13-15)

The blind men in Jericho—Two blind men sitting by the roadside were begging for food. (Note to self: back in those days if you were blind you had big problems. Not only were you likely very poor, but you were snubbed because your blindness was assumed to be the result of a sin you or your parents had committed.) They heard a ruckus as a crowd gathered. There was talk of Jesus being in town. As the frenzy reached its height and they realized

Jesus was near, these two men started yelling to get his attention: "Son of David, have pity on us." To make a long story short, he did and they were able to see. Normal day: Grace became visible; they responded; they were changed. (Matthew 20:29-34)

Are you sensing a pattern here? Three steps:

- Normal Day: praying on Sunday, begging and being ignored, suffering from a chronic illness.
- I notice Gods' grace: the rumbling crowd, the guy preaching, glimpse him passing by.
- I respond: baptize me, heal me, let me see!

Let's take a clue from these stories. Our NTHs and problems are opportunities that can set the same pattern in motion. On any normal day, we can choose to notice God's grace and respond.

Consider the experiences and encounters of your normal day. Are you all wrapped up in comparing yourself to your sibling? Is that same kid sitting alone at lunch again? Are you holding on to a grudge so firmly that you are becoming bitter and quick-tempered? Does lying seem like the only way to get attention? Like our Biblical forerunners, **you can notice God's grace present in the opportunities and obstacles of your normal day and respond.** Go to the ULC and say with confidence, "Lord, I know you're with me. Help me to think about this situation differently. Heal me! Let me see!"

God is able to make every grace abundant for you,
so that…you may have an abundance for every good work.
2 Corinthians 9:8

Grace is like rain. It's abundant and everywhere. Soak it up.

1. In what situation or relationship do you want to be able to notice and respond to God's grace?

2. Name two of your peers or older teens who seem to be working at finding God in their lives. In the days ahead, look for opportunities to thank each of them for being an important person of faith for you.

Begin with the Sign of the Cross and ask Jesus to be with you.

Imagine that you are a character in the story of Jesus and the blind men in Jericho. Try to create the town in your mind. See the buildings and dirt roads. What time of day is it? What is the weather like? Where exactly are you in the scene? Notice all the people and activity around you. Hear the chattering, gossiping and calling out.

Suddenly the crowd grows louder and you sense that Jesus is about to walk by.

What do you do to get his attention?

He notices you and stops.

What do you say to him? What does he say to you?

Before he turns to continue on his way, thank him for his wisdom.

Watch Jesus make his way through town.

When he is out of sight, end your prayer with the Sign of the Cross.

Chapter Thirteen

Safety Check: How's My Thinking?

So you're on your cross-country expedition in your well-stocked SUV. You're traveling over hill and dale. You've seen rainy conditions, terrible heat and humidity, pot-hole stricken back roads, and reduced oxygen in the upper altitudes. Every day before setting out on the next leg of the journey you give the vehicle a quick 5-point safety check and fix any potential problems. You want to be sure the vehicle is in good condition before you commit to the next 600-mile day on the road.

Folks on the PATH take this advice out of the *Cross-Country Traveler's Guide to a Successful Road Trip* and apply it to their brain, the 'vehicle' that is leading them every day. The next set of habits you need for the journey will allow you to recognize potential problems and resolve them before they become big issues. **If you begin the day with these safety checks, you can assure yourself that the Emperor isn't on board and waiting to pounce from the get go.**

"Say what? How can I perform a Safety Check on my brain?" You can perform a simple test before even getting out of bed and then again throughout the day at convenient times. It's the most powerful tool of personal responsibility and awareness that you have at your disposal. You'll want it close at hand. **The Line** will help you gain awareness of your state of mind, mood and attitude.

The illustration to the right will help here. The vertical line is the Ruler. It measures the quality of your thinking: the mood you are in, your state of mind, your general attitude, your level of energy, your perspective on the day ahead. On the Ruler are plotted the various mental states a person can experience, from positive to negative.

Above the Line

- A positive view on life and how I see the world.
- My thinking is effective and yielding good outcomes.
- I'm working on being hooked into God and in the yoke with Jesus.

Below the Line

- A negative view on life and how I see the world.
- My thinking is unreliable and ineffective.
- I am in danger of Letting Other Stuff Triumph.
- Depressing moods and emotions.

The horizontal line is simply 'the Line.' It represents the difference between Above the Line (ATL) thinking and Below the Line (BTL) thinking. When you are **Above the Line your thinking is serving you well and bringing out the best in you.** Those healthy and effective neural synapses are really snapping. When you are BTL your thought patterns expose you to danger. **Below the Line you are at the mercy of Negative Thinking Habits and pessimistic moods** and, therefore, a prime target for the Emperor.

Awareness and the Line

We all spend time both ATL and BTL, whether we are on the PATH or LOST. It's normal to have highs and lows. Thinking patterns and perspectives can change daily and even throughout the day. In fact, the hormones your body produces sometimes cause those shifts to take place.

The major difference between PATH and LOST folks is that **those on the PATH know these shifts take place and impact their thinking and perspective.** So they self-check their position on the Line regularly.

Let's assume you are on the PATH. Taking a moment to gauge your position on the Line makes you aware of what's going on in your head. When you are aware, you are alert and powerful. You can approach your day and the people in it mindful of what you are bringing to the party—both good and bad. If you don't like where you find yourself on the Line, you can actively work at moving up. If those efforts fail, you can choose to protect the people around you and remain Below the Line with dignity until you are able to get back Above the Line.

When you are on the PATH, no matter where you are on the Line you are in a position of power. If you are BTL and struggling because you can't improve the situation (for example, a sickness in the family), you still know you can work on your attitude and move up the Line by improving your experience from the inside out. Even Below the Line you know that **it is easier to change your thinking habits than it is to change things outside yourself** (parents, teachers, school, and job). You'll use all the tools available (more on that ahead) to direct yourself to an ATL experience.

> "You cannot tailor-make the situations in life but you can tailor-make the attitudes to fit those situations."
> –Zig Ziglar

This drives EE crazy! He can't get at you because you refuse to give over the power of your thoughts and attitude to him. Rather than following his temptations to blame others or make excuses for being BTL, people of the

PATH dig in and take *more responsibility* for their lives, preferring to yoke up with Jesus in the ULC and create a new perspective rather than taking a bite out of an apple made just for them.

Your Choice: Master Your Problems or Be Mastered by Them

On the PATH or LOST, this one life you've got to live is going to come with problems and trips BTL. It's not to be avoided. The question at hand is this: how will you handle those problems and those trips?

Daily ups and downs pretty much handle you if you are LOST. You begin to view life as unfair and out of your control. As a result, **you allow your problems to take you BTL.** Your overriding way of looking at life ("It happens to me " or "It's out of my control because I Let Other Stuff Triumph") leaves you feeling powerless. Your thought patterns wall you in with planks. You can't get Above the Line because the way has been blocked by negativity and your submitting cheer: "I am a Victim!" Rather than work to free yourself from this pitiful navel-gazing, you submit to the Emperor. **You give away all your power.**

Being LOST is seriously miserable!

When on the PATH, problems become the fuel for increasing your Virtue Quotient (VQ). Would more self-control and focus improve that attitude in math? Would confidence help you feel more comfortable around your sick grandparent? How about some teamwork and tact on the ball field? Rather than give away your power by blaming or making excuses, you look at yourself and say, "All right, then. There's work to be done and planks to be moved. To the ULC!"

True, when you are BTL you must first do the work of moving ATL since it is difficult to effectively problem solve from Below the Line. If you are on the PATH, you know this and get to the business at hand. **You exert control and power over your situation,** thereby becoming a worthy opponent to the Emperor.

Indicators, Invitations, and Submarines

Your road trip vehicle has warning lights that let you know when the airbag is disabled, the on-board computer needs rebooting, or the emergency brake is engaged. Similarly, your brain and body send signals that you are Below the Line. These are called **Indicators,** the feelings you have or the behaviors you exhibit when you are Below the Line.

Indicators are person-specific. They don't come in a one-size-fits-all format. How do you know when *your* thinking is not working in your best interest? Check the Indicators you experience when your thinking is not working effectively and leading you BTL:

Emotional Indicators:

- ☐ anger
- ☐ frustration
- ☐ impatience
- ☐ feeling inadequate
- ☐ forgetfulness
- ☐ envy
- ☐ self-doubt
- ☐ sadness
- ☐ other______________

Action Indicators:

- ☐ yelling
- ☐ judging
- ☐ fighting
- ☐ arguing
- ☐ sarcasm
- ☐ putdowns
- ☐ withdrawal
- ☐ other______________

Physical Indicators:

- ☐ fatigue
- ☐ nervous fidgeting
- ☐ shortness of breath
- ☐ rapid heartbeat
- ☐ tightened muscles
- ☐ other______________

Your Indicators can help you to identify your **Invitations,** the events and circumstances that increase the odds that you will slip Below the Line. When you first become aware of an indicating signal, *pause and think.* What just happened? What is going on? What happened that caused these signals to start blinking? Pinpoint the cause. Are any of these Invitations for you?

- ☐ Being sick, in pain, or overtired
- ☐ A pet peeve—the sound of chewing, slow walkers, constant sniffling
- ☐ Getting behind in your work or doing poorly on an assignment
- ☐ Being shut out of a seat at your usual lunch table
- ☐ A referee making a call that goes against your team
- ☐ Knowing somebody laughed at you because of something you said
- ☐ A parent telling you that you can't do something you want to do
- ☐ Other______________

Everyone has his or her own set of Invitations. *These are the EE's access point into your soul.* If you are off guard, an Invitation will get out of control in a hurry and lead you not only BTL but also into hurting other people. This, obviously, is in direct conflict with your purpose (to be good to other people in God's name) and directly aligned with the Emperor's purpose (to thwart God's Grand Design).

So you're on the PATH and you realize that an Invitation is causing you to slip BTL. You are determined to get Above the Line as quickly as possible. You are also determined to protect other people from yourself while you are in this not-so-healthy state of mind. So you employ another strategy: the Submarine. An ocean-going submarine is designed to keep you safe underwater (no oxygen, too much hydrostatic pressure, white sharks in the vicinity). In PATH language, **a Submarine protects you and others when you are BTL and a possible danger.** It's a simple tool that works beautifully and is much appreciated by everyone around you. To get in your submarine all you have to do is let people know you are BTL (or feeling down or cranky or struggling or needing to be alone for a while) and you will resurface when you have worked through the gunk and won't hurt anybody with your words or behaviors. Then you set about the business of getting back ATL without fears of hurting other people while you are BTL.

TRUE TALES

One of my 'Teacher Invitations' is when students sabotage themselves by not living up to their potential. This Invitation was delivered one afternoon when several students came wildly underprepared for their final project—the Demonstration Speech.

Presentation dates had been assigned a month ahead and several weeks of class time had been devoted to writing, rewriting, practice performances, and peer review. As the third presenter went down in flames, my pulse quickened, facial expressions stiffened, and arms crossed tightly over my chest. The class was on the edge of their seats waiting for my reaction, expecting the worst.

Knowing this was only an Invitation helped me to protect my class from a teacher tirade. Instead, I talked about my true disappointment over students making choices that lead to failure rather than success. Rather than witnessing an angry rant about laziness, my students saw a Submarine employed.

Trampolines

Sometimes you don't get strong Indicators and no Invitations are apparent. Perhaps you just wake up BTL and on the wrong side of the bed. No matter how you fall Below the Line, you'll need another skill to move back Above the Line. A **Trampoline** is a technique that helps you to refocus your thinking and recalibrate your brain, thereby bouncing you back ATL.

Your strongest and most reliable Trampoline is strapping up in the yoke next to Jesus and asking Him for help getting back ATL. It's never easy to avoid temptations or keep from giving into strong emotions. The EE is counting on you ignoring this Trampoline, trying instead to fix it on your own. But honestly, that's just another little reenactment of The Fall. Going directly to some other option first means we are still focused on our own power to save ourselves. Reaching out for grace doesn't mean we give up our own power; it means we admit that we are only powerful enough when we are finding our strength in God. While the Trampolines that follow can help you bounce, they will be less effective if you haven't first reached out to the grace that is all around you.

Here are some common Trampolines that can help get your thinking Above the Line. Which do you use?

- ☐ Physical exercise or playing outside
- ☐ Listening to music
- ☐ Talking the situation over with a friend or trusted adult
- ☐ Playing with young children
- ☐ Performing an act of service
- ☐ Doing projects: making, mowing, cleaning, building
- ☐ Removing yourself from the situation
- ☐ Journaling, drawing, dancing
- ☐ Being kind or grateful
- ☐ Other____________________

Remember: reaching out for grace should be everyone's first Trampoline. A simple "Help me, Lord!" will do. Beyond that your Trampolines will be unique to you, and they may change with time, experience, and use. Experimenting with different options is highly recommended. Gentlemen, you may smirk at the idea of baking, but there just may be a curative chef within you! For all you introverts out there, who knows? Maybe getting outside yourself by visiting folks at a nearby nursing home will help to lift you back up ATL.

1. You have the power to live more frequently Above the Line and to visit only briefly Below the Line.

   - What *Invitations* influence you to move BTL?
   - What *Indicators* (feelings or reactions) alert you that you are BTL?

2. Remember what you can do to move ATL when you are BTL:

   - Turn to Jesus immediately for support and guidance.
   - Use your favorite Trampolines.
   - Take responsibility and change your thinking.

Offer this prayer just before you go to sleep this evening.

Pray the Sign of the Cross and then ask Jesus to come and be with you.

Choose the Invitation that is most problematic for you.

Close your eyes and imagine sitting with Jesus on a bench at your favorite park, beach, or other place in nature.

Spend some time telling Jesus about this Invitation. Explain why it is so easy to be set off by it. Share a real-life example.

Then rest in his presence for a bit, confident that he wants to help you.

Pray the Sign of the Cross before you sleep.

Chapter Fourteen

Thought Circles

A powerful Negative Thinking Habit called the Thought Circle (TC) is a regular visitor to the LOST brain. Thought Circles develop rapidly and often drag us BTL in a heartbeat or two. They can be stubborn to disarm and potentially destructive to both yourself and your relationships. It makes sense, then, that they are a favorite technique employed by the Emperor. His goal is to disrupt your true purpose. A Thought Circle will spiral you deep inside yourself, knock you out of the yoke with Jesus, and hurt either you or someone else. Since we all get LOST sometimes and because TCs work so effectively in blocking our PATH, they merit a chapter of their own.

When you are experiencing a Thought Circle, one negative thought rapidly leads to another and another and another, like a snowball gaining speed and size as it hurls down the face of a mountain. Sometimes the thoughts link together logically. Sometimes they ricochet all over. If you recount a thought chain to an objective listener, she would say, "You're nuts."

Thought Circles present themselves in one of two types: the Worry Thought Circle and the Anger Thought Circle. Girls often gravitate toward the first, boys toward the second. Though not a scientific fact, plenty of evidence suggests that your gender is linked to your Negative Thinking Habits. But I'll save that for another book!

The Worry Thought Circle

Can any of you by your worrying add a single second to your lifespan?
Why are you anxious?
Matthew 6:27-28

What might a Worry TC look like in real time? Here's a for instance:

That chain of thoughts took approximately 48 seconds to whip itself into a frenzy inside Cecelia's head. Certainly, by the time she was halfway through the process, her BTL Indicators were lighting up all over the place: scowl on her face, arms crossed, angry pacing, and elevated heart rate. The Emperor had wound her up and wound her up good.

It's wise to have an early detection system for developing Worry Thought Circles. Be on the lookout for these traits:

- They take place rapidly.
- They are littered with highly judgmental, unfounded thoughts (planks).
- They often include catastrophic, worst-case scenarios.
- They undermine our own well-being by bringing stress, anxiety, or unnecessary doubts.

The Worry Thought Circle will primarily wreak havoc within you, as the above list suggests. It keeps you from thinking clearly about the situation, resulting in feelings, actions, and outcomes that send you even deeper Below the Line.

The Anger Thought Circle

Be angry but do not sin; do not let the sun set on your anger, and do not leave room for the devil.
Ephesians 4:26-27

What a fantastic Bible quote! Anger is *not sinful.* It has a place and it has a purpose. But it needs to be brief (hence, don't let the sun set on it) and it needs to be alert to the Emperor's attempt to manipulate it. Anger can easily become a weapon for inflicting pain on another person. It can also be directed toward yourself.

Imagine Trent is watching TV downstairs when he hears his dad calling from upstairs .

Trent's heated outburst reveals both the similarities and differences between Anger and Worry TCs. Anger Thought Circles:

- Take place rapidly.
- Are littered with highly judgmental, unfounded thoughts (planks).
- Result in significant losses for you (no game, in this example).
- Trigger anger, retaliation, or hurt in other people (see dad's reaction above).

Not only has the Emperor seeped into Trent's heart, but his anger helped EE find a crevice to slither inside his dad's heart. Just a handful of seconds and the impact was made, leaving much lost and much to be repaired.

The two-fold impact of the Anger Thought Circle keeps you from thinking clearly and serves as an Invitation to others to fall BTL.

Stop Thought Circles in Their Tracks

It is easier to corral an Anger or Worry Thought Circle when it is just beginning. This is true of all Negative Thinking Habits. Once full-blown and out of control they are much more difficult to rein in. This takes us back to the importance of awareness. *Awareness is your ally.* **If you are aware of what you are thinking and of your primary Invitations and Indicators, you will be able to apply the brakes when the downhill slide to Below the Line first begins.** Your thinking is easier to control when it is just beginning to accelerate rather than moving like a runaway train.

But let's say a thought gets away from you and is on its way to becoming a full blown Worry or Anger Thought Circle. What now?

The **Not Now** technique interrupts the faulty thinking patterns that instigate and feed Thought Circles. When you catch yourself beginning the negative spiral, say, "Not now. This is a Thought Circle." Saying it out loud is especially effective. Repeat it to yourself as necessary. Naming it for what it is takes much of the wind out of its sails and may just give you the pause you need to regroup and take control of your thinking. Don't worry about how you look to others. People walk around talking on Bluetooth all the time. You'll fit right in.

The Not Now technique works well on unfounded worries and angers. However, sometimes a concrete basis exists for your worry or anger. Perhaps your family is dealing with a health crisis or job loss. When a situation like this occurs, you need to first evaluate if you are Above the Line and have the time to deal with it effectively in the present moment. If you do, then go for it. But what if you are in class or studying for a mid-term that's tomorrow? What then?

When you are unable to give a thought or problem the time and attention it requires, you can put it in a mental **'Parking Lot.'** This is a metaphor for the temporary storage of distracting thoughts until they can be addressed effectively. You can just set the thought aside for a while and concentrate on what must be done in the present moment. You aren't ignoring it or pretending it doesn't exist. It will, most definitely, be waiting for you when the more immediate concern is over. So go ahead and make an appointment with it. You will be able to give it your complete Above the Line attention at that time. As a result, you will be better equipped to deal with it in a way that is respectful and proactive, thereby bamboozling the Evil Emperor's efforts to sway you once again.

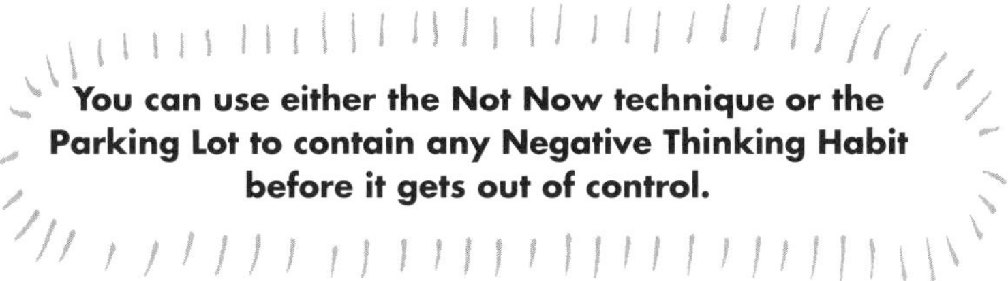

It's All in the Good Book

We destroy arguments and every pretension raising itself against the knowledge of God, and take every thought captive in obedience to Christ.
2 Corinthians 10:5

Ummm...say that again?

It's one of those Bible moments. The good book has an important lesson to teach us, but we need to take the time to figure it out. What do all those words *mean?* To get a true understanding of this passage, we need some clear definitions. Look! I've found them for you.

Destroy: to put an end to
Pretension: a claim usually not supported by facts
Knowledge: information
Captive: to prevent escape
Raises itself against: questions
Obedience: to follow guidance

Using these definitions, we'll rewrite the passage in a clearer way:

We put an end to arguments and every unsupported claim
that questions the information of God,
and we keep every thought from escaping
so that we follow the guidance of Christ.

When it comes to Thought Circles, the Bible was all over it about 2,000 years ago (approximately 55 A.D.) when the second letter of Corinthians was written. Obviously, those folks experienced the same circles we do. Based on the Bible quote, it also seems obvious that they knew **awareness was their ally.** They used the Not Now and Parking Lot techniques to control their thoughts. They definitely saw the importance of keeping their eyes turned to God rather than in on themselves, as the Emperor wishes.

The Bible tells us in a nutshell: Reach out for Grace. Stop the anger. Stop the imaginary ideas. Don't let your thoughts spin out of control. Stick to God's law. Follow Jesus's teaching.

1. Are you more likely to become angry or to become worried?

2. Think of a time recently when you were either angry or worried. Let yourself remember the situation and the accompanying emotions and then practice using both the Not Now technique and the Parking Lot to take control of the feelings. Which tool is more effective for you?

Pray the Sign of the Cross.

Ask Jesus to be with you right now and to help you feel his grace.

Now that you know which Thought Circle (Anger or Worry) you are most likely to experience, read the corresponding Bible quote below a few times.

> *Worry:* "Can any of you by your worrying add a single second to your lifespan? Why are you anxious?"
>
> *Anger:* "Be angry but do not sin; do not let the sun set on your anger, and do not leave room for the devil."

Which portion of the quote stands out for you?

That is Jesus's grace breaking through.

Write that part of the quote in your homework planner or on the back of your hand to help you remember it today.

Thank Jesus for his guidance.

Close with the Sign of the Cross.

CHAPTER FIFTEEN

Confronting NTHs and Temptation:

Tools For In The Moment (ITM)

In spiritual terms, your NTHs are your temptations. **Temptations are the Negative Thinking Habits that penetrate at the vulnerable spots of your soul.** Think of them as small rips in the fabric of a hot air balloon. As long as that rip persists, your balloon will have trouble rising. If you leave the rip unattended, it will grow larger and more troublesome, eventually grounding you completely.

Knowing that we live in a grace-filled world, however, is all the hope we need for mending these rips.

St. Paul reminds us, "I can do all things through Christ who strengthens me." (Philippians 4:13) God, through Christ, has filled the world with every grace and strength that you need for confronting and controlling your temptations. This is **The Law of Opposites.**

THE LAW OF OPPOSITES:
For every temptation there is a virtue.

The antidote for any NTH or temptation can be found in a virtue. For example:

Use these Virtues	To defuse this NTH or Temptation
Love, Compassion	Jealousy
Self-control, Focus	Boredom
Forgiveness, Mercy	Holding a grudge
Responsibility, Diligence	Procrastination
Empathy, Patience	Sarcasm

Consider the hot air balloon as a metaphor for your soul. Virtues have the power to repair rips, resist future punctures, and strengthen the integrity of your soul's fabric, thus preventing new rips from occurring. The more virtues you acquire, the stronger your VQ. The stronger your VQ, the stronger the fabric of your soul.

The perpetual availability of these virtues allows you to go to battle against your temptations and defuse their power. This is not to say that applying the Law of Opposites, building your VQ, or mending those rips will be easy. But how would it change your life if your temptation was reduced in size by 80%? Would your family, your school, or your team be different if you were tackling your NTHs by increasing your VQ?

How can you do this in a practical and effective way? It begins with a commitment to **Name It, Claim It, Tame It.** This strategy gives you the tools you need to work though NTHs by identifying them, taking responsibility for them and doing something about them.

Name It means that you are aware of and name your NTHs and Planks: "I'm being selfish" or "I'm feeling jealous."

Claim It means that you take responsibility for your thought or feelings: "I'm responsible for being selfish…feeling jealous." If you don't claim responsibility for your thoughts, feelings, or actions, then you can't change them. You are likely to blame someone else for what you are experiencing. However, by claiming them, you also claim the power to change them.

Tame It means that you take specific action to stop the thought, feeling, or action. *When you decide to tame an NTH or temptation, you actively begin practicing a virtue.* The stronger you grow in that virtue, the more you are able to reduce the NTH.

You saw how Name It and Claim It work when you learned about tackling Thought Circles. Both Not Now and The Parking Lot are effective naming and claiming strategies. By using them,

- the thought is identified and
- you acknowledge that it is your responsibility to control and reframe it.

Mastering the Art of the Stop

While it may seem obvious and easy, stopping a Negative Thinking Habit is neither. Our days are busy and our thoughts are relentless. **Monitoring your thoughts and recognizing when one of your NTHs is bubbling up is a skill that you will need to commit to for a lifetime.** You should expect that gaining initial traction in this area will demand persistence and resilience. It will grow easier over time and you will develop a method that serves you well if you stick with it.

As you begin practicing the Art of the Stop, you will find it tremendously helpful if you simultaneously begin practicing the habit of tapping into God's grace all around you. Say out loud or in your heart a phrase as simple as "Stop now. Grace like rain." With that phrase you jiggle the plank by turning away from yourself and toward God. You will feel God with you immediately. Really. A new perspective will result.

So it may not be easy, but it is manageable and you are not alone.

Once you have stopped and tapped into grace, you can apply taming techniques until you find one that is effective. You'll know it's effective when you are able to see from a different perspective, move Above the Line, or find yourself curious about the situation, rather than needing to be right.

It's time to collect some solid strategies for taming NTHs. They will be grouped in two sections: **Tools for In the Moment** and **Tools for After the Fact.**

Tools for In The Moment (ITM)

Some temptations and NTHs thrust themselves upon us like icy patches on the PATH. They present sudden, unanticipated challenges to our pursuit of all things holy, tempting us to choose EGO (Edging God Out) over loving God fiercely and completely by being good to others.

These sudden attacks by the Emperor demand powerful responses that can be used immediately and produce swift results. The following strategies offer just the help you need. Pack Rewriting and Monitoring Chit-Chat in your suitcase for the PATH, along with Not Now and the Parking Lot.

Rewriting: Remember writing something and then realizing that you could write it better? So you erased what you wrote and rewrote it a better way. You have the power to do the same thing with your thinking. You can 'erase' your thoughts and 'rewrite' them again. Two methods of Rewriting are available to you.

1. *Turn It Inside Out.* One way to rewrite your thoughts is to turn them inside out. You can do this by taking the initial thought and literally rewriting it into an opposite form. Here are some examples:

Instead of: *"I've always been like this."*
How about: *"I don't want to be this way forever. It stinks."*

Instead of: *"She's the one with the attitude problem."*
How about: *"I might be getting an attitude problem."*

Instead of: *"It's too hard. I'll never change."*
How about: *"It's not easy but I can change."*

Rewriting asks you neither to lie nor to pretend you are living in a fantasyland. Instead, **it allows you to let some light in from a different angle by trying on other ways of thinking.** It jiggles the plank a bit and gives you a new way to look at a problem.

2. *Be Curious.* Do you have a sudden death grip on a seriously negative thought? Is that thought leading to seriously negative results? Inserting the words "I wonder," "Maybe," "Perhaps," or "What if" into your rewrite can help loosen it up. The Holy Spirit can work wonders with these words, if you are open to it happening. For example:

"Learning algebra is pointless," turns into
"I wonder what Virtues will help me get through this class."

"I can't believe I trusted her," turns into
"What if I try to forgive her?"

"Mr. Bleakbeak is so mean," turns into
"Maybe there is something I don't know about his situation."

Curiosity opens all sorts of doors and can literally expel a plank on contact. No longer do you feel trapped in a negative situation that is spiraling out of control. Instead, possibilities and options are open to you. For the first time you might realize that a teacher's bigger life can affect your classroom interaction with him. Learning how to forgive other people, in the end, teaches you the truest meaning of love in the book. Reframing a less than ideal learning situation as an opportunity to develop a virtue for the PATH is about the finest anti-Emperor strategy ever!

Monitor the Chit-Chat Inside Your Head: Group work can be a great thing when everyone is working ATL and bringing their personal skills to the task.

When we focus our energies on a common goal the final product is far more awesome than what we can produce on our own. Sometimes, though, group dynamics can be difficult. If we have competing ideas about how to approach the project, we can get off on the wrong foot from the get go. If we aren't good listeners, other group members may feel slighted. If we are lazy, we can be an Invitation for someone else's anger.

Trying to defuse a NTH can feel like a really bad group work situation because one of the voices at the table is the Emperor. When you are thinking from a negative perspective, the EE will immediately pull up a chair for a chat, smooth talking and painting a picture of how right you are, or how much easier it would be to do it your way.

Let's say you are bored in a classroom. The chit-chat inside your head might sound something like the following:

You may think this is just you talking to yourself, but is it? If you reframe this self-talk as a conversation with the Emperor, you'll realize that you are being played. His sole purpose is to EGO (Edge God Out) and in the case of boredom he often does it by encouraging us to judge and belittle other people.

How do you stop the chatter? **Remember: awareness is your ally.** As soon as possible interrupt the conversation by asking inside your head, "Who's talking?" If you need to, write it in the margin of your notebook or text it to yourself. By asking the question, you jiggle a plank and reveal what is going on: **you are being tempted.**

Now you can shift your thinking from "This is so lame" to "I'm so tempted" and that frees you to redirect your thoughts. Perhaps you are still bored in the classroom, but you can take control of the boredom and exert some power over it. Maybe you'll challenge yourself to pay very close attention for the next ten minutes. Maybe you'll force yourself to ask a good question about ant life. Maybe you'll choose to sit by Martha next class because she is clearly not bored and you can try to follow her example.

What you won't do is engage in an internal conversation that is leading you Below the Line (BTL) by Edging God Out (EGO).

Rewriting and Monitoring Chit-Chat, by the way, work for all sorts of NTHs. Procrastination, jealousy, self-doubt, pride, and fear of failure all respond well to these techniques.

1. You can master the *art of the stop* by becoming aware of what is going on *just before* you experience a temptation. Follow this process:

- Name the temptation you want to control.
- Identify real examples of when this temptation got the best of you.
- Write down what was taking place in each example *just before* it entered your mind.
- Look for patterns and recurring Invitations in the examples.

2. Identifying Invitations and patterns will help you *name* and *claim* your temptation ahead of time and allow you to *tame* it before it can control you.

3. Which tools for *taming* In the Moment are you willing to try?

Start with the Sign of the Cross and ask Jesus to be with you and help you feel his grace.

Bring your temptation in #1 above to mind. Say an Act of Contrition.

Review the Build Your VQ Chart on page 23 and identify 2-3 virtues that can help you defuse this temptation.

Close your eyes. As you inhale, repeat the name of the virtues. As you exhale, breathe out the name of your temptation. Do this for a few moments.

Rest quietly and ask the Holy Spirit to help you grow in these important virtues.

Close with the Sign of the Cross.

CHAPTER SIXTEEN

Confronting NTHs and Temptations :
Tools For After The Fact (ATF)

Some Negative Thinking Habits and temptations are especially powerful because they are woven into our memories and behavior patterns. For example:

- Comparing ourselves to siblings can lead to discouragement, resentment or dishonesty.
- An embarrassing or hurtful childhood memory can lead to a lack of self-confidence or deep shame.
- Not experiencing success in school may lead to apathy, anger, or hopelessness.

These types of long-term NTHs don't respond well to In the Moment tools because they are woven deeply into our life stories. Uprooting them requires regular reflection that is built into an ongoing, step-by-step, After the Fact (ATF) action plan. As you learn about the ATF tools in the pages ahead, imagine applying them to a deeply rooted NTH or temptation in your own life, though you will need them all in your PATH suitcase.

Confronting NTHs After the Fact is deeply meaningful work because it frees you from the EE's most powerful grip on your soul. When you decide to do this work, set yourself up for success by staying Above the Line and tapping into grace.

Law of Conviction

I grew up believing I was not very smart. My two older brothers were crazy smart and if my homework was too hard I turned to them for help rather than trying to figure it out on my own. They earned high test scores and scholarships and I could never match them academically or live up to their achievements. No matter how hard I worked, they would always be better than me. I was convinced.

Thoughts like these that begin with absolutes ("I'll never…," "They always…") present a special challenge to de-planking. An NTH held with deep conviction can leave you so planked in that you cannot even imagine thinking differently. This is the Law of Conviction.

> **LAW OF CONVICTION**
> The more we believe something to be true, the truer it feels for us.

De-planking an absolute thought begins by plotting the strength of that thought on the Conviction Scale. Try it yourself. Pick an NTH that is a strong temptation or significant problem for you. For example, "My teacher hates me" or "My brother got all the luck in the gene pool." On the Conviction Scale below, place an 'X' on the number reflecting the strength of this thought. That's your level of conviction.

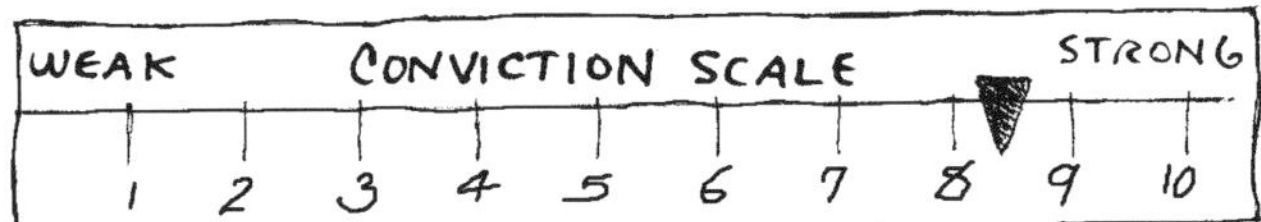

Easing Up

When you find yourself gravitating to the right side of the Conviction Scale, it can be difficult to address your temptation or NTH In the Moment. You may be too deeply stuck in gunk. The **Easing Up** process invites you to thoughtfully devise concrete methods for reducing your strong NTH. You'll need to take two distinct actions:

1. **Be Curious.** Rewrite your NTH using one of the key words: Maybe, What if, I wonder, or Perhaps. When you rewrite in this way, you don't remove it completely, but experiment with turning down its intensity.

2. **Take Small Steps.** Identify concrete behaviors you can practice that will help you to move the scale slowly to the left. This sets you up to see success more quickly in smaller increments. Step by step success will help convince you that this NTH can be tamed.

How might Easing Up look in real life? Let's consider Franklin. Franklin believed his English teacher hated him. His conviction of this belief was an 8. Because this was his *thinking,* he *felt* anxious about going to class, wasn't *doing* his homework, and was *getting* a poor grade. (The Frame in action.) Determined to ease up to a 5 on the Conviction Scale, Franklin started by rewriting his belief to "Maybe my teacher hates me." In addition to the rewrite, he decided to jot down all the negative comments his teacher made during the next two classes.

Franklin made a huge realization. Based on the negative comments he collected, it occurred to him, "Maybe that's just how my teacher is. He's that way to everybody. It might not be just about me." Having been successful in reducing his conviction to a 6 with this strategy, Franklin decided to keep it up for the next week. Later, he realized that his conviction had dropped to a 3.

Another example involves Lauren who was bombarded with negative messages about her physical appearance when she first came to high school. Two classmates in particular wouldn't let up. Though Lauren tried to ignore their hurtful remarks, eventually they started eating at her. She found herself believing what they were saying and began scrutinizing her looks constantly. Her level of conviction was off the scale (10+) and she needed relief.

Lauren rewrote her belief to "What if I don't need to fit into anyone's idea of beautiful but my own?" Her concrete steps included:

- Removing the mirror from her school locker.
- Throwing away the fashion magazines she had saved up in her room.
- Saying "Not now" when comparing herself to other girls in class.

After a few weeks of concentrated effort, Lauren found herself a lot happier with both her appearance and her life. Negative Thinking Habits were no longer causing her to obsess about the outside while letting the inside deteriorate. When she felt in control of the NTH, she even replaced the mirror in her locker. It made her proud to look at herself and know she was ATL and thinking clearly.

The chart below offers some helpful tips for Easing Up in various situations. Refer to it when you are trying to ease up on an over-the-top conviction to a Negative Thinking Habit or temptation.

When you recognize a strong negative thought or belief:	If you find yourself actually trying to prove that the belief is true:	Try on a lower Conviction Level
Name it: "This is a really negative thought!"	Insert "Maybe" or "I wonder if" at the beginning of the thought.	Identify one or two actions that match a reduced level of conviction.
Shut it down by saying "Not Now!"	State the exact opposite of your thought; challenge your belief.	Practice those actions for a concrete amount of time.
Put the thought in a Parking Lot in order to rein it in.	Ask an objective, trusted friend or adult to help you evaluate the truth of the thought.	When time is up, look for evidence of lower conviction. Set new action goals; begin again.

Review Your Videos

Most professional athletes study the videos of their practice sessions and competitions. Whether batting, dribbling, blocking, skating, or tumbling, they are looking to increase their success by reducing their weaknesses and, in so doing, get a leg up on the competition.

Like a professional athlete, **when we are on the PATH we spend time looking at our problem areas and reducing them with discipline, thereby getting a leg up on the Emperor.** We're working to be more successful in the future by learning from the past.

Folks . . . athletes are playing sports. They play games with sticks, balls, skates, and beams. Yet these athletes offer us a most excellent After the Fact strategy for identifying and weeding out our NTHs and temptations: Review Your Videos. At the end of each day, look over how you did. Take special notice of your weaknesses so you can reduce them tomorrow.

The Five Steps: What might a typical Review of the Videos look like? The following step-by-step plan is based on the Examen, a spiritual exercise created by St. Ignatius Loyola about 500 years ago. (*See Faith Sidebar*) Millions of people on the PATH have used his formula to identify their planks and ward off the advances of the Emperor.

Born to a wealthy family, Inigo de Loyola was spoiled and vain about his looks. He was a ladies' man, a troublemaker, and had a police record for brawling with intent to inflict serious harm. He joined the army for adventure, but his leg was struck by a cannonball during battle. Still wanting to look good in tights (seriously!), he endured a series of gruesome, unsuccessful operations which left him with a limp.

Bored during recovery, Inigo began reading a book about saints. He was captivated by their spirit and courage, and felt profoundly called to be like them. So began his remarkable transformation from spoiled young soldier to a man after God's own heart.

Over the next 30 years, Inigo founded the Society of Jesus (an order of priests commonly known as the Jesuits), wrote a masterful handbook of spirituality, opened schools, and sent missionaries throughout the Western hemisphere.

Almost 500 years later, you are learning how to use his Examen. Pretty awesome for a guy who once was way too concerned about his tights!

- ☐ **Step One: Tap into Grace.** Remind yourself you are in God's grace at this very moment. You have nothing to fear or worry about. You are yoked up to God who is ready to look at your day with you.

- ☐ **Step Two: Say Thanks.** Let your day flow before you. It doesn't need to be chronological. What were the highlights of this day? Focus on the goodness and blessings. Who made you laugh? Any unexpected surprises? When were you most relaxed? At what point did you feel most free of worry or stress? What virtues did you see yourself using today? Thank God for all the goodness!

- ☐ **Step Three: Fast-forward Do Over.** Start at the beginning of your day and try to see yourself in each room, class, vehicle, field, and situation. You don't need to spend a lot of time in any one place. The most important task is to see the people who were there in each situation. Take mental selfies of your day as if you are planning to update your social media. These pictures will help you recall what was taking place in each situation and what you were thinking, saying, and doing. (This step takes the most time and the most practice to do well. You'll get faster and better with practice.)

- ☐ **Step Four: Sorry. Forgive Me.** Nobody is perfect and the Fast-forward Do Over helps us to call to mind our sins in the yoke next to Jesus. With him close at hand we can apologize, ask for his forgiveness, and even listen for suggestions or guidance. There's no need for shame or embarrassment. God already knows the temptations that were a problem for you in this day and is waiting for you to name them, claim them, and begin to tame them. Which brings us to…

- ☐ **Step Five: Grace for Tomorrow.** Tomorrow is another day and you are going to face similar temptations and NTHs when it gets here. So start asking God *now* to help you see and respond to grace tomorrow. Then say good night and let yourself sleep peacefully, knowing that God is watching over you.

Set Yourself Up To Succeed. As mentioned before, folks have been using forms of the Ignatian Examen for almost 500 years. Lucky for you, that means the following tried and true tricks are available to help you be successful.

- ☐ **Manage Your Expectations.** It will take a little while to get into the Video Review swing. Research suggests most new habits require 21 days to really take root. Challenge yourself, but give yourself the time you need. Your NTHs didn't develop overnight and probably won't be quickly transformed into virtues.

- ☐ **Build in Consistency.** Most habits stick because they become a part of a routine. How can you fit the Examen into your night? You might try adding one step to each part of your bedtime routine. For example:

- Change clothes = Tap into Grace.
- Straighten room = Say Thanks.
- Brush, Floss and Rinse = Fast-forward Do Over.
- Wash face = Sorry. Forgive Me.
- Lights out = Grace for Tomorrow

☐ **Individualize Your Routine.** If bedtime doesn't work for you, what does? Is there a place in your house where you feel most relaxed? Do you prefer to write? Do you think clearest on your feet while moving? Know your nature and learning style and create a routine that respects them both.

☐ **Frame Your Review.** These last precious moments at day's end are a second chance for you to see God's presence and invitations to you in the day behind. There is no reason to see this as a display of your mistakes. **The Review is about God's grace, mercy, and complete devotion to you.** So stand in the ULC and ask for help seeing how God's presence was woven into your day, whether or not you initially noticed.

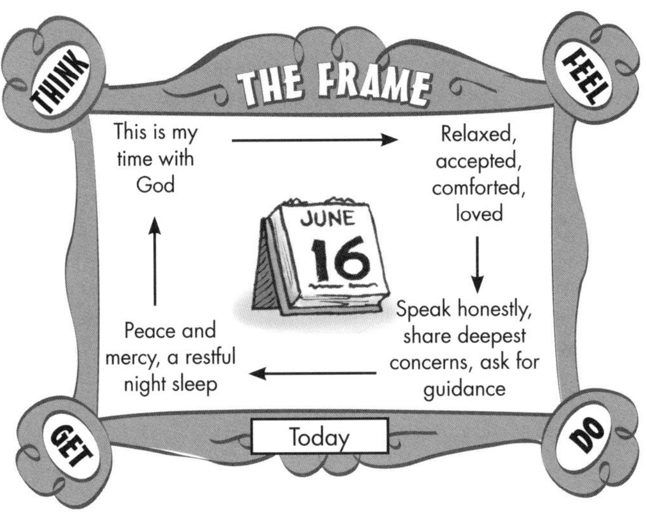

The Crucial Halftime Report

We can compare our nightly Examen to timeouts in a basketball game. Did the opponent just drop four baskets unanswered? Take a time out. Do we want to slow down the pace? Take a time out. Is there a play that would work perfectly here? Take a time out. At the end of the first quarter there is an official two-minute break. Players water up, pump each other up, and catch their breath.

Then, of course, there is halftime. Teams go to the quiet and privacy of their locker rooms where they settle down and talk about how the game is going.

Give and take conversation takes place. They pinpoint the opponent's strengths. They look at their own weaknesses and see how the opponent is manipulating them. Players own up to the mistakes they've made. Solid advice is offered and a game plan is put in place. A strong pep talk revs everyone up for the second half. Then, they get back on the court to play again.

Hmmmm...sounds pretty similar to a powerful Sacrament.

The Sacrament of Confession or Reconciliation is that all-important 'halftime' for people of the PATH. It's the ultimate After the Fact strategy. We're playing a crucial game on a much bigger court and our opponent is mega-skilled. We're taking timeouts as often as we can, (every night when we Review Our Videos) but that isn't going to be enough. We need halftime.

During the precious moments of this sacrament,

- We review our days and discuss our weaknesses.
- We are offered solid guidance.
- We receive forgiveness and the amazing blessing of God's sacramental grace.
- We are sent back out on the PATH .

Our 'halftime' confession is the ultimate act of tapping into grace. We say, "This is what I've done. I'm so sorry. Please take it away." With great mercy God does just that. It's as if a tidal wave of grace envelops us, washes away all that had EGO, and turns us back toward the Garden. There's a reason we feel so good when we leave the reconciliation room after an honest confession. **We have been reconciled After the Fact.**

Lessons for Your Lifetime

Collecting virtues by confronting temptations and Negative Thinking Habits doesn't just make you more effective in the present; it sets you up for a smoother journey on the PATH. Just as establishing strong neural pathways in your brain right now will benefit your future schoolwork, career, and relationships, the same can be said with regard to the Virtues. Learning to persevere through a tough class now will help you persevere through a vexing problem at work in the future. Learning to be patient with an irritating sibling now will prepare you to raise your own children with patience in the future. Practicing stepping into and stopping an ugly chain of gossip now will enable you to confront loose-lipped libel in the office or even in your church or home when you are an adult.

In the Moment and After the Fact strategies will help you build the skills you need to swap out NTHs and swap in Virtues. They are concrete skills you can use to confront the very real temptations created **just for you** by the Emperor.

Remember: character and virtue don't just happen. You pursue them by doing the work of aligning your free will with God's Will and getting back to the Garden.

1. Rate the strength of your greatest temptation or NTH on the Conviction Scale.

WEAK CONVICTION SCALE STRONG
1 2 3 4 5 6 7 8 9 10

2. Identify two specific actions you will use for one week in order to reduce that conviction by a few points.

3. Set up a strategy for Reviewing Your Videos. Be sure that:

- It fits in your schedule.
- The setting is comfortable.
- The routine is easy to remember.
- You check the level of conviction of your temptation or NTH during your review.

Find out when your parish offers the Sacrament of Reconciliation. Work with your parents and choose a convenient time to get to Church this week and receive God's grace through this Sacrament. Encourage your parents to receive the Sacrament as well.

CHAPTER 17

The Land of Other People

We've spent pages and pages considering Part One of your Purpose: to know and love God deeply and fiercely. Focus has been on connecting you to the truth about who you are in God's eyes and challenging you to engage in a life-altering intimate relationship in the Yoke. You've begun honing and harnessing your thinking skills and are learning the habits of a strong sense of self-awareness, which is the ultimate tool you need in your suitcase while on the PATH. At the same time, you've begun to address the very real presence of evil by learning to recognize it at work within yourself (ewwwww… sounds like a worm) and practicing strategies to combat it.

This inner work is the job of a lifetime. No matter where you live, what career you pursue, whether you choose to marry or not, Job #1 remains. While some jobs are a burden, this job is Our Purpose. As Catholic Christians we know we are able to be successful at this work because we know we are swimming in grace all around. In fact, the Catechism (see sidebar for the direct quote!) reminds us **we received all the grace we need to pursue our purpose at our Baptism.**

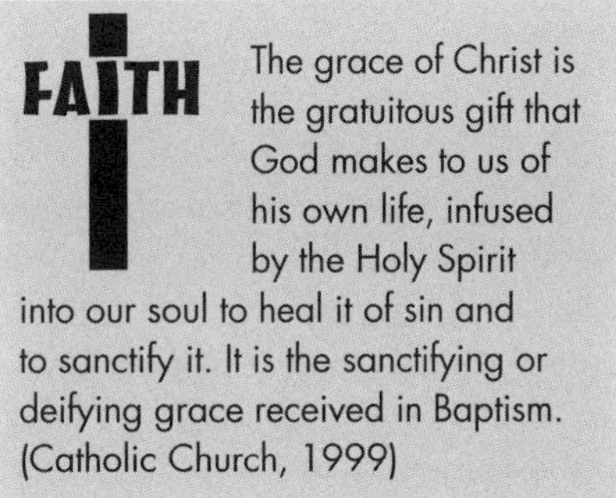
FAITH

The grace of Christ is the gratuitous gift that God makes to us of his own life, infused by the Holy Spirit into our soul to heal it of sin and to sanctify it. It is the sanctifying or deifying grace received in Baptism. (Catholic Church, 1999)

And Here's What the Catechism Means

Why baptism? We humans need signs to help us negotiate our way through life. When you go to a ballgame at a stadium you follow the signage to your ticketed seat. Traffic lights and stop and exit signs direct us while driving. Airports spend thousands of dollars on signs directing us to our gate, to our arriving passengers, to return our rental car, and to baggage claim.

Baptism is God's sign. After The Fall and the passage of several thousand years spent trying to get back to the Garden, it was apparent that we could not figure out how to overcome real evil (the Emperor) and our own limitations (NTHs and Temptations). Baptism is like the flashing neon light we needed that said, "This Way Home." **By way of our Baptism, God reaches out to us through human things (water, oil, garment, candles, and community) to help us understand that grace and guidance are all around us, everywhere.**

It works like this:

- Baptism fills us with sanctifying grace which gives us the power to believe in, hope in, and love God, completely and fiercely.
- Baptism removes all our sins, including that tragic Original Sin that took place in the Garden.
- Baptism wraps us completely within the person of Jesus and the Holy Spirit makes a home in us.
- Baptism gives us a family to walk the PATH with—the Church.

In short, we are claimed inside and out for God, filled with all the grace we need to find our way home, every obstacle to success is removed, and we're even introduced to folks who are making the same journey. **Since Baptism is God's sign, it not only tells us where to go, it is where we need to go.** The visible water of the font really washes us with the invisible waters of grace.

***All of history* led to God ultimately coming to us as a human so that this outward sign of Baptism, this road map home, could be given to us.**

True enough, the journey is still challenging. As humans we will always struggle with a tendency towards sin. You know it and I know it. You feel it and I feel it. Temptation is real and can be very inviting. Sometimes we are weak and sometimes we choose to turn away from God. The Catechism calls this tendency "concupiscence," and way back in 1546 Church leaders referred to it as "tinder for sin." If you've ever built a fire you know what tinder is. It's the stuff you lay at the bottom of the heavy logs because it easily ignites (dry twigs and sticks, pine needles). That way you can get your fire going in a hurry. That's what this tendency towards sin is. It's easily sparked if we aren't on our guard against temptation.

FAITH

From the Catechism: "As a result of original sin, human nature is weakened in its powers, subject to ignorance, suffering and the domination of death, and inclined to sin (this inclination is called "concupiscence"). (Catholic Church, 418)

The Good News is that there is always forgiveness and God's mercy and reconciliation. That's the promise of your Baptism. Sin is taken away and the road back to the Garden can be cleared over and over again. You can get home.

What about All These Other People?

Much of what we've been talking about in this book has to do with the first three aspects of Baptism—grace, being loved by and loving God, and dealing with our sinful nature. The fourth aspect of Baptism remains to be considered. We also become members of the Church and therefore **members of each other.** The Church calls this the Mystical Body of Christ. If you look up mystical in the dictionary it says: "having a divine meaning that is beyond human understanding." Well, yes and no in regard to the Mystical Body of Christ. Certainly we will never be able to conceive how it is that God is able to dwell within each of us intimately and yet simultaneously. That's just way outside the human ballpark of understanding. Still, a few things are completely understandable when we compare the Body of Christ to the human body.

Thing One: Get In Shape An athlete at the top of his game will tend to all parts of his physical wellness because he knows that excellence results from proper training and preparation. A marathon runner may appear to be primarily using his legs for his event. However, he will carefully monitor his hydration throughout training and competing to ensure adequate oxygen transfer between blood supply and internal organs because those organs power his legs. Core muscles will be built up in order to support form and technique during the grueling lengthy runs. Special attention will be paid to callouses, corns, and nails of the feet (seriously) to remove friction and prevent blistering. Many marathoners practice visualization to ready their minds for late-mile hills and the infamous 'Wall' often experienced around mile 20.

Legs . . . internal organs . . . core muscles . . . feet . . . brain. For the marathoner's body to function at its peak all the individual parts need to be in tip top shape.

So too with the Body of Christ. For the Church to function at her peak, each of her members needs to be 'in training.' Each of us needs to be in the yoke with Jesus and on the PATH with our GPS set for doing God's Will. We need our thinking and vision to be clear (de-planked) and set on the road of discipline, and we need to be building our VQ through self-awareness and determination. These are the demands of Job #1. **We are members of Christ's body. Working at getting ourselves into tip-top shape is our daily task and our primary duty to everyone around us.**

Thing Two: Do Your Part The human body works precisely because the members function harmoniously, relying on each other to provide their gifts. Nothing can stand independent of the rest. While your legs propel you across a field, your eyes watch out for divots and roots to avoid. When you eat, teeth chew and your tongue forces food into a pipe that contracts to force bulk down to the stomach. The stomach pulverizes the food, releasing nutrients small enough to pass into the blood system which delivers them to hundreds of organs that each carry out a life-sustaining function. In the meantime, the intestines take the trash out. Take away one of these workers and the system breaks down.

Comparison of worth doesn't take place within the body. The parts don't busy themselves trying to show each other up with coolness and they do not suffer from the evils of envy by wishing they were something other than what they are. What they are is necessary and important, with each part tending to its own tasks and assisting other parts as needed. If all the parts wanted to be eyes, we'd be one sorry looking human body!

What should be your take away from this? **When you find yourself envying someone else's gifts or abilities, arm yourself with a single phrase: "Compare and despair."**

Thing Three: Help Others Get There Remember Part Two of your purpose? You are to be good to others in God's name. The human body gives us a few lessons in what this looks like as well. It offers example after example of selfless service:

- When the back itches, the hand scratches it.
- The heart beats to move oxygen to all other parts.
- Legs bear weight to transport the rest of the body from place to place.
- Fingers make food in order to sustain the whole.
- When one arm breaks, the other arm assumes its responsibilities until the break heals.
- When bleeding starts, an army of clotting agents stops its flow. Meanwhile, white blood cells destroy bacteria poised to enter and cause infection.

No whining. No cries of "That's not fair." No excuses. No blaming. No complaining that "It's too hard," "It's not my job," or "I can't make a difference." The parts do what needs to be done for the good of the whole. They step in to offer extra support when a crisis is happening with no paybacks expected. **The parts serve each other.**

Certainly, God chose the concrete and instructive metaphor of the human body to help us understand the Grand Design for creation and the meaning of True Happiness. This isn't a solo journey on the PATH. God means for us to find our way back TOGETHER. But why? Because **our efforts to move along the PATH connected to each other, working with each other, and helping each other reveals the kind of love that GOD IS.** God IS love and has made each of us as a reflection of that love. When we live our True Purpose, we love. **When you use your desires, passions and gifts to treat others well in God's name, you live your purpose and you help the rest of us see God.**

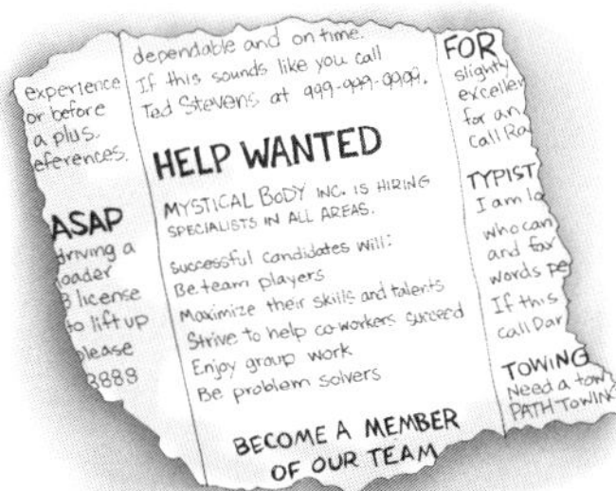

We travel the PATH as the Mystical Body of Christ, with Jesus giving us direction, purpose, and leadership. We cannot remind ourselves too often that God took on a human body and showed us how to be human. Jesus did this by speaking a language we can understand, no matter the language we speak.

Jesus spoke the language of ACTIONS: Heal. Forgive. Feed. Listen. Teach. Comfort. Pray. Challenge. Sacrifice. Serve. And he did it in the Land of Other People.

Guiding Principles in the ULC

This brings us to the final section of our text: The Land of OP. Whether on the PATH or LOST, we all live in the Land of Other People. Unless you have a distinct vocation to become a hermit living in a cave, your days are going to be filled with people, people, and more people. As wonderful and energizing as folks and relationships can be, they can also be overwhelming and frustrating.

As a person of the PATH you know there are a few **guiding principles in the Land of OP:**

- **Power Within:** The biggest influence on the quality of the countless interactions you have with all these people is how you think and act. Happily, as you have learned, this is under your control and direction. Even more powerful is the truth that **you are in that Yoke with Jesus and he will help you think and act your way through these interactions with grace and God-like style,** if you stay in constant contact and follow his lead.
- **God of Many Yokes:** While on the PATH, you begin to comprehend that God is somehow able to be totally devoted to each individual human who seeks Him. Every resident of the Land of OP is loved by God in a head-over-heels way and it is God's desire to be yoked up to each one. In the quiet, wonderful moments when

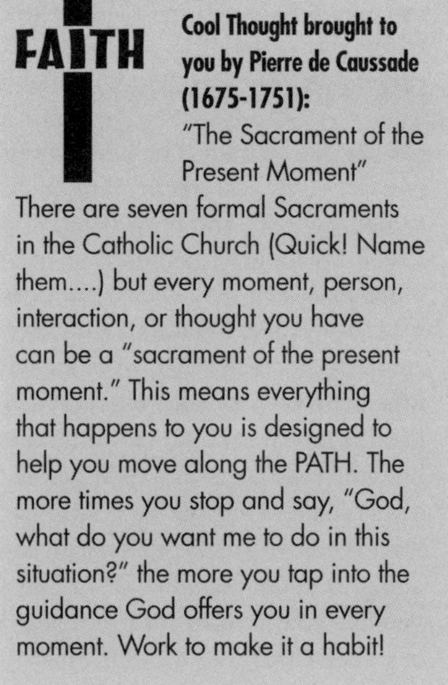

Cool Thought brought to you by Pierre de Caussade (1675-1751):
"The Sacrament of the Present Moment"
There are seven formal Sacraments in the Catholic Church (Quick! Name them....) but every moment, person, interaction, or thought you have can be a "sacrament of the present moment." This means everything that happens to you is designed to help you move along the PATH. The more times you stop and say, "God, what do you want me to do in this situation?" the more you tap into the guidance God offers you in every moment. Work to make it a habit!

you experience how much God loves you—despite your sins and NTHs, despite the times you took Him for granted or forgot to be thankful, despite *everything*—you come to understand that **God showers mercy and love on all the people of the Land of OP.** God has enough for everyone. Because you have firsthand experience of what it's like to be caught up in God's awesome love for you, *you* wish that type of experience for *everyone else.*

- **Opportunity for Others:** When you PATH in the Land of OP, you come to trust that **whatever and whoever comes into your life offers an opportunity to take a step towards God's will for you.** Every person and situation, both positive and negative, is an opportunity for you to learn about, grow closer to, and be shaped by God. The flip side of that coin is this: **you are an opportunity for others to step closer to God.** By sharing the landscape of the Land of OP, we are challenged to move towards God together.

A person of the PATH brings these principles to the Upper Left Corner of the Frame and our discussion of the Land of Other People will be guided by them. Knowing God seeks each citizen in the Land of OP creates a universal responsibility: **we have a fundamental obligation to help each other get back to the Garden.**

We are one body and the way back to God is connected to each other.

It's a Mess out There

On a typical spring day in the United States the national weather map can be marked by extreme heat in the Southwest, soaking rains in the Northeast, tornadoes throughout the Midwest, and high winds diving across the Great Lakes. Forest fires in California, flooding along the Mississippi, and drought in the Deep South can occur simultaneously, while the upper plain states enjoy abundant sunshine and Hawaii's weather is perfect.

Like the weather map, the Land of OP is a really messy place. Jesus used the parable of the sower to teach us about this mess:

> *A sower went out to sow. And as he sowed, some seed fell on the path, and birds came and ate it up. Some fell on rocky ground, where it had little soil. It sprang up at once because the soil was not deep, and when the sun rose it was scorched, and it withered for lack of roots. Some seed fell among thorns, and the thorns grew up and choked it. But some seed fell on rich soil, and produced fruit, a hundred or sixty or thirtyfold.*
> *Matthew 13:3-8*

On the PATH

How can we use this parable as instruction for our journey on the PATH through the Land of OP? We can understand the sower and his seeds as Jesus and the yoke he offers each of us. But what of the rocks and choking weeds, the scorching sunshine and drought, and the predators that devour the seed? One way to frame them is as the challenges we will meet along the way on the PATH. We will face envy, anger, rejection, disappointment, and loss. Every day will bring its bumps and bruises.

We can get all uptight about the mess or we can look to the example of Jesus for our inspiration. That cross was a big, tumultuous 'mess' involving excruciating pain, heroic obedience, and selfless sacrifice. But it was transformed into Resurrection and the sending of the Holy Spirit, which led to our baptism and the way back to the Garden.

While none of us will ever bear a cross like his, each of the challenges in the Land of OP can be framed as **a mess loaded with the potential for transformation.** If approached with Jesus in the yoke, you can use every challenge to reach a deeper understanding of yourself and of Jesus, while building life-skills that will serve you in the next challenge, and virtues that will strengthen your soul for the long term.

THINK ABOUT IT

1. Evaluate yourself as a citizen in the Land of Other People. Shade in a portion of each bar graph, thereby indicating how well you are fulfilling your responsibilities.

Get In Shape

0%						25%						50%						75%						100%

Do My Part

0%						25%						50%						75%						100%

Help Others Get There

0%						25%						50%						75%						100%

2. Who do you know that is all three: in shape, doing their part, and helping others?

Begin with the Sign of the Cross.

Ask Jesus to be with you in this prayer time.

Focus on one of the people in #2 above.

Bring to mind some favorite memories you have of this person.

Thank Jesus for putting this person in the land of OP with you.

Ask Jesus to bless and strengthen this person for another day on the PATH.

Close with the Sign of the Cross.

Chapter Eighteen

Building Your Trust Fund

As you travel through the Land of Other People, it won't take long before you realize that those closest to you are the people in whom you place the most trust and whose trust you have earned.

I trust you  You trust me

This is important. The Land of OP is a messy place, filled with all types of influences and attractions, lures and invitations, potholes and panoramas. Just as a shrewd baseball general manager bargains and trades to create a top notch starting lineup, people on the PATH make thoughtful and wise choices about those who become their closest companions and mentors as they navigate their way through the Land of OP. **They surround themselves with folks who share similar values and are working toward the same goal: finding True Happiness by using all that God wove into them to do His will.**

In the pages ahead, you will learn how to build essential friendships, identify mentors, and maximize your family ties. **Trust is the essential virtue that will allow you to maintain all of these powerful and important relationships.** This is where you start skill building.

The Trust Fund Metaphor

It's a no brainer that the most important ingredient in any relationship is **trust, the firm belief in the honesty and reliability of another person.** Since it is the crucial component in a solid relationship (whether friend to friend, child to parent, employee to employer, or boyfriend to girlfriend), you need to strengthen your skills in being a trustworthy companion.

In his book, *The Seven Habits of Highly Effective People,* Stephen Covey introduced the concept of the Emotional Bank Account to visualize how trust is built up and lost in a relationship. His idea is adapted here and called the **'Trust Fund.'** It operates like a bank account.

Let's say you mowed lawns over the summer. Each week you made $120 and every Friday you deposited that money in your bank account. At the end of the summer you had saved $1200. You wanted to upgrade your smart phone, so you withdrew $250 from your bank account. That left you with $950.

Like a bank account, we make deposits into and withdrawals from our Trust Funds. The goal is to keep your funds 'in the black,' with the deposits well outweighing any withdrawals you might make. The more trust you keep in the fund the more likely the other person is to give you the benefit of the doubt. Disagreements and conflict arise in every relationship, but if they are few and far between and your Trust Fund is full, rough patches are easier to work through.

Kindness Deposits	Unkind Withdrawals
Saying "Thank you" and "I love you"	Being sarcastic
Smiling or saying hello as you pass someone in the hallway	Excluding or ignoring someone
Giving a sincere compliment	Ridiculing or laughing at someone
Introducing yourself to a new student	Judging people based on looks
Telling the truth	Cropping out in order to publicly blow someone off
Keeping promises	Lying
Speaking well of those who are absent	Breaking promises
Apologizing	Talking behind another's back

TRUE TALES My daughter and her high school boyfriend were conscientious about making deposits in their parent Trust Funds. They spent lots of time hanging out with us, always came home on time, helped with dinner dishes and spoke openly about challenges and difficulties they faced at school and on the weekends. They built up a lot of credit. When they made an unfortunate withdrawal over bad choices that they owned up to before getting caught, they had enough left in the Trust Fund to keep its balance in the black. It was a rough patch, but easy to work through.

Deposits

Four types of deposits are guaranteed to build every Trust Fund. Your parents will appreciate them as much as your best friend. They are hallmark habits of people on the PATH: kindness, truth telling, promise keeping, and apologies and repairs. When you make these sorts of deposits you are also building up your Virtue Quotient. As we look at each one we'll consider which virtues are being strengthened with every deposit.

1. Practice Random (and Planned) Acts of Kindness: Pick up a friend's cleats and carry them to the locker room when you notice his hands are full. Empty the dishwasher while your mom is out or do it before she asks. Buy your little sister a sucker when you stop off for a soda on the way home from school. Thank your teacher for that day's lesson, even if it wasn't the greatest.

Kindness is a deposit because it says, "I noticed you." Even the most well-rounded, optimistic people can experience loneliness and self-doubt, and depression and isolation are tremendous crosses for some people. Because we do not know the interior state of everyone in the Land of Other People, the habit of meeting each one with kindness is certainly the best policy to follow.

You have probably heard the Bible story of Zacchaeus and Jesus. But do you know what really happened that day?

> *Now a man there named Zacchaeus, who was a chief tax collector and also a wealthy man, was seeking to see who Jesus was; but he could not see him because of the crowd, for he was small in stature. So he ran on ahead and climbed a sycamore tree in order to see Jesus, who was about to pass that way. When he reached the place, Jesus looked up and said to him," Zacchaeus, come down quickly, for today I must stay at your house."*
>
> *Luke 19:2-5*

When a gospel writer gives a detail, it's usually for a reason. In this case, the detail that Zacchaeus was a tax collector is a critical element of the story. Tax collectors were Jews who worked for the oppressive Roman government. Their job was to ensure that the Jewish people paid every cent of their way-too-high-to-begin-with taxes to Rome. Tax collectors were *hated* by everyday Jews. They were considered traitors to their race and slimy good-for-nothings. As if that wasn't enough, Zacchaeus was really, really short. He probably was made fun of and mocked for his stature as well.

The fact that Zacchaeus was desperate to see Jesus, running about and hanging out of trees to get his attention, suggests that he was not completely proud of his own choices. Maybe he was hoping that this miracle worker he'd heard about would be able to help him change his ways, too.

What did Jesus do? *He noticed him.* "Zacchaeus, hurry and come down, for today I must stay at your house." There, amid the crowd that mocked, ridiculed, and hated Zacchaeus, Jesus publicly extended a warm invitation to him, and one that was filled with kindness. **Like Jesus, you will be practicing the virtues of empathy, compassion, and generosity when you take the time to notice and reach out to others with kindness.**

Jesus spoke the language of action: be kind. You are called to make those same types of deposits.

2. Truth Telling: No deposit is more central to building trust than telling the truth. Practicing truth telling from the get-go in even the smallest of situations is of great importance. It builds a strong foundation for you to stand upon when the Evil Emperor tempts you with fabricating a story, misleading, or omitting truths in bigger circumstances. And you will be tempted!

As with any skill, you get better at truth telling with time and practice. Building a habit of honesty in minor situations will give you the courage to speak the truth in tough situations. Plus, **the habit of truth telling strengthens many other virtues, including self-discipline, respect, and integrity.** Any negative consequences are far less severe than the hefty withdrawals associated with lying, covering up, and being found out.

The truth telling that Jesus did often upset people—usually people in power like the Scribes and Pharisees. For example, when on trial before Pilate, Jesus told him, "For this I was born and for this I came into the world, to testify to the truth." (John 18:37) Occasionally, you will be challenged to stand up for the truth in tough situations. You may feel the Holy Spirit nudge you to defend someone being made fun of in the locker room because, the truth is, no one should be tormented in that way. Or, you may know the real scoop behind what went down in the back row during the test and, the truth is, denying it when the teacher challenges the class about it is pretty sinful. These are tough situations that ask you to challenge your peers with the truth. But the world is in desperate need of people who are brave enough to testify to the truth.

Jesus spoke the language of action: tell the truth. You are called to make those same types of deposits.

3. Promise Keeping: When you tell your parents you will call at 8:00, call at 8:00 if not five minutes early. When you tell a neighbor you will babysit, don't cancel the morning of the appointment. When you tell a study group you'll have your section complete for the work session, show up with the work in hand.

When you give your word in a promise, you are entering into a type of covenant, or bond, with another person. If you break your word, you break your bond. Each time you keep a promise you strengthen your bond with that individual. **You also strengthen your ability to PATH by building virtues of dependability, honor, and responsibility.**

Jesus did this all the time. He told the Roman centurion that his son would be healed, and his son was healed. (Matthew 8:5-13) When Jesus told the crowd that the official's daughter wasn't dead but sleeping, sure enough, she woke up. (Matthew 9:24-26) Jesus forecasted Peter's three denials; that happened, too. (Mark 14:30) He said he would send the Holy Spirit to be with us. (John 14:16) Check. The list goes on and on.

Jesus spoke the language of action: keep promises. You are called to make those same types of deposits.

4. Apologies and Repairs: Let's state up front that this is a type of deposit Jesus never had to make. There was no "tinder toward sin" in him. He had no need to be forgiven and no mess to fix after making a withdrawal from a Trust Fund. He did, however, say things like, "If you bring your gift to the altar, and there recall that your brother has anything against you, leave your gift there at the altar, go first and be reconciled with your brother." (Matthew 5:23-24) Basically, Jesus was giving us good solid relationship advice: take responsibility for the problems you cause, rebuild trust, and be at peace with

each other. **Apologies and reparations allow you to build up the virtues of humility, courage, and empathy.**

As Adam and Eve portrayed so clearly, it's just a fact that where there are humans there is going to be sin. Withdrawals will occur between even the best of friends. Offering a genuine apology with an honest admission of your faults is a huge deposit. We all know how hard it is to admit we were wrong. We all know what it is like to feel guilt and shame. We also know that Jesus was all about forgiveness and mercy and bringing people back to the PATH. Put all of this together and it makes for one heck of a deposit when we say, "I'm sorry. Please forgive me."

The power of a heart-felt apology cannot be overstated. If you apologize after you offend someone, you begin to restore trust. The further step of making repairs requires you to fix what is broken. Broke the vase? Came in after curfew? Passed on a rumor? Your apology is reinforced when you work to make amends. Perhaps you find a way to replace the vase, or come in 15 minutes ahead of curfew for a couple weeks, or fess up to the person you shared the rumor with that it wasn't true and you shouldn't have passed it on. Making repairs is *work*, but if you are looking to make deposits in a Trust Fund, it is extremely effective.

You are called to speak the language of ACTION: apologize and make repairs.

What's It Worth?

The value of a deposit is determined by the receiver of the deposit, not the giver. For this reason, it is important that you determine what the high value deposits are for people who are important to you. For instance, you can say to your mom, "I love you," you can empty the dishwasher, and you can offer no complaint when she asks you to run to the grocery store for a few things while she is making dinner. Consider your mom. Which deposits mean the most to her? Give it some thought and then make a conscious effort to make the type of deposits that she values as often as possible.

A final word about withdrawals: Any withdrawal of trust from a relationship is a serious matter. Depending on the severity of the withdrawal, numerous deposits may be necessary to make up for the trust lost. Do not be surprised to learn that **one deposit does not necessarily equal the value of one withdrawal.** Think about it from your own experience. If a friend you trusted breaks that trust by sharing one of your secrets with others, will a simple spoken apology restore your trust? Most likely not. You will need plenty of deposits before you again consider sharing important information with that person.

1. Which deposit is hardest for you to make: Kindness, Truth Telling, Promise Keeping, Apologizing or Repairing?

2. Which of your Trust Funds currently needs major deposits?

3. Identify three deposits you want to make into one of these Trust Funds. Write them into your planner or leave a note on your bathroom mirror reminding you to make these deposits.

Pray the Sign of the Cross and ask Jesus to be with you.

Talk with Jesus about the type of deposit that is hardest for you to make. Explain why it is challenging.

Describe a time when you tried, but just couldn't make the deposit.

Ask him to be with you the next time an opportunity for this type of deposit presents itself.

Then spend some quiet time listening.

Close with the Sign of the Cross.

CHAPTER NINETEEN

Building Trust With Parents

The four hallmark deposits (kindness, truth telling, promise keeping, apologies and repairs) are important for building trust with anyone. When building a Trust Fund with your parents, there's something else you need to understand.

Most of the things parents and kids argue about are Little Things, stuff like curfew, cleaning your room, doing homework, or taking out the trash. **These Little Things are important only because they are attached to Big Things.** Example: if you want to come home at 12:00 a.m. and your parents want you in at 11:00 p.m., midnight is a Little Thing. The Big Things are your desire for independence to make your own choices and your parents' need to know that you are safe.

The Law of Big Things

Big Things are those things that are most important to us. **If you and your parents help each other get the Big Things, your relationship will be smoother and more satisfying.** If either of you doesn't get these Big Things, your relationship will be rocky and stressful.

You understand the Big Thing for you: Space. It's important to find the balance between staying connected to your parents and having Space to be independent. You need Space to do your own thing and make your own decisions. You need Space to grow up and experience life beyond your own yard. This desire is natural and necessary. It's your built-in vocation to become who you are meant to be in the Grand Design. It's called freedom.

Although you understand *your* Big Thing very well and your desire for it, you may not understand *your parents'* Big Thing: Peace of Mind (POM). To understand how your parents feel about you and your well-being, consider this example. Think of your most valuable possession (your smart phone or iPad, for instance). How would you feel if that item were left amid a crowd of strangers in a place you are uneasy about for five hours this Saturday night? It could be stolen, damaged, or misused. Wouldn't you be concerned about what might happen to it? That is the same feeling that your parents have when they drop you off at the mall with friends on a weekend night.

Your parents love and care for you far, far more than you care for your phone or iPad. They feel deeply committed to the awesome job of keeping you safe and on the PATH until you are able to navigate the Land of OP on your own. **Because you are in a transition time (brain development, habit building, learning to de-plank, VQ growing), they find themselves both hanging on and letting go.** Parents need to *hang on* to best assure your safety and they need to *let go* to enable you to move along the PATH.

The big takeaway for you is this: **when your parents feel that you are safe and growing in VQs, then they will have Peace of Mind.**

> **THE LAW OF BIG THINGS**
>
> Teenagers need Space and parents need POM.
> Parents give Space only when they have POM.
> When parents give Space and teenagers handle that Space responsibly, parents have greater POM.
> With greater POM, parents give more Space.

Breaking the Law of Big Things has consequences.

- If parents give Space and you don't handle it responsibly, parents lose POM and tend to limit Space.
- If parents don't give Space, you may tend to rebel. Rebellion reduces parents' POM and they tend to restrict Space even more.

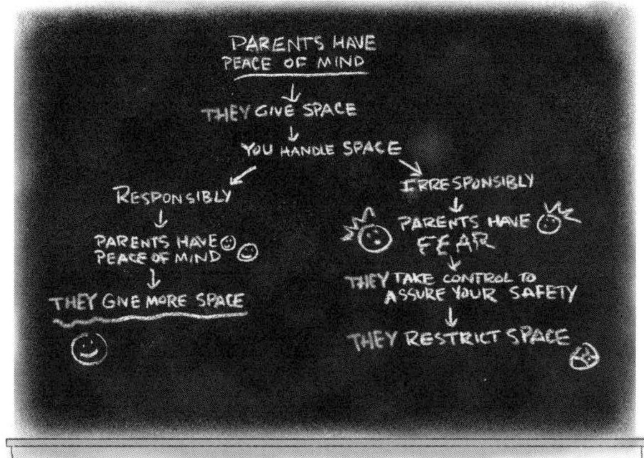

You can bolster your parents' POM in regard to your safety in numerous ways. Some examples include:

- Getting home on time.
- Letting them know where you're going and calling if you go somewhere else.
- Bringing friends over so your parents can get to know them.
- Texting when you arrive safely at your destination.

How do you give your parents Peace of Mind in regard to your VQ? **Show them virtues in action.** Here are a few suggestions:

- Ask their advice when you find yourself in a difficult situation.
- Accept fair consequences without attitude or complaint.
- Be responsible to your calendar and commitments.
- Avoid the use of jokes that demean others.
- Notice when a sibling is struggling with homework and help out.

Think about the Virtues you are determined to strengthen within yourself. **Every concrete effort you make to build up your VQ will increase your parents' POM.**

Your Decision

Because you were blessed with Free Will, you have a choice in how you approach getting your Big Thing. You can create a revolutionary war within your home or you can do whatever you can to maintain your parents' POM while pursuing your Space. Consider these two points as you decide:

1. The Fourth Commandment: One of your responsibilities is to the Fourth Commandment: honor your mother and father. While some situations make this honoring and the obedience it asks of you challenging, most of the time yielding to the guidance and wisdom of your parents is in your best interest. They have much to offer you for your journey on the PATH.

2. The Mystical Body: God has willed it that we travel this Land of Other People together. We are responsible for each other. The best way to make the journey successful for all is by helping each other get the Big Things.

Working together, you can achieve Space and your parents can have Peace of Mind. Along the way you will learn to listen well, ask questions respectfully, and speak openly with each other. These are skills built on virtues that will help you be successful with your future friends, spouse, and co-workers.

It's worth the effort to dedicate yourself to pursuing the Big Things with your parents now. Making the investment helps you create the habits that enable you to build important relationships in the Land of OP.

1. What have you done recently that has increased your parents' Peace of Mind and, in turn, your freedom?

2. What have you done recently that has reduced your parents' Peace of Mind and, in turn, your freedom?

Pray the sign of the cross and ask Jesus to be with you right now and to help you feel his grace.

Identify 2-3 happy memories you have of being with your parents. Recreate and enjoy them again in your mind.

In your heart offer a spontaneous prayer for your parents. Talk to Jesus about them. Be as honest, grateful, and humble as you know how to be.

Finally, ask Jesus to guide you as you strive to honor them and increase their POM.

Close with the Sign of the Cross.

Chapter Twenty

Co-Travelers: Friendship

"When all is said and done,
if you can count all your true friends on one hand, you're lucky!"

To you of the social media generation the above quote may seem rather lame. "What? Only five friends? I have 1,247!" Indeed, I have a friend of similar age as me who kept herself up late one night begging Twitter users to get her over the 10,000 followers threshold.

In a world of friend of a friend of a friend 'friends,' and 'friends' found on Facebook, imagining yourself with only a handful of friends when all is said and done is a bit of a shocker. Though technology offers us the opportunity to create friendships with a click of a button, the human heart was built for intimate relationships—close, personal friendships that carry us through good and bad times alike. Relationships such as these are few and far between and, truly, can be counted on one hand. Choosing those friends is a seriously important undertaking. Why? Read on.

It's a beautiful world out there. Creation itself is all the reason we need to rejoice. You can explore it on skis, with snorkels, on camels, bike or foot, overhead, and underground. You have a career to look forward to, perhaps a spouse to marry and a family to raise. You'll have opportunities to travel, to taste foods of many cultures, and to learn endless new skills or languages. The Land of OP is a treasure chest of possibilities.

But it is also a field filled with landmines. The briefest unguarded Google search can land you in places both immoral and embarrassing. Fashion, television, movies, and music all have the power to create beautiful things or they can be used by the Emperor to lull you into thinking that 'anything goes and anything's good.'

Do not be led astray: Bad company corrupts good morals.
1 Corinthians 15:33

People on the PATH know who made them (that would be God) and what they were made for (to know and love God fiercely and to be good to others in God's name). They know that landmines and temptations are a part of the terrain. So they make a simple but powerful decision that helps them stay on the PATH while traveling in the Land of OP: **they decide to surround themselves with friends who help them to stay on the PATH.** Their friends strive to increase their own Virtue Quotient. They work to make the right choices in difficult situations. They tackle problems with determination and dedication. They make deposits on a regular basis.

You are on the PATH. Over the course of your lifetime, your best friends (those you'll count on the fingers of one hand) will be the people who helped you to travel safely through the Land of OP, and you will have done the same for them.

Your best friends will be the ones who challenged you to stick to the PATH and find True Happiness by staying in the yoke with Jesus.

Deeper Deposits

Once you make a firm commitment to a true friendship, a new set of deposits can deepen the quality of that friendship. It's these types of deposits that become the roots of a lifelong relationship.

Know Their Stories: Listen with real concentration when they tell you about the stuff going on in their lives. Concentrate on the story line. Ask questions to

make sure you understand the facts and details. Really understand what they are telling you, where they are coming from, and what they have been through.

Challenge Them to Stay on the Path: We all get angry on occasion. Things irritate us, people disappoint us, and even the closest of families go through difficult times. **When your friend shares these types of situations with you, your challenge is to offer responses and feedback that can *only* lead them to the stay on the PATH.** What does this mean? It means you can't rile them up, get swept up in their anger, or feed any negative thoughts with your own negative thoughts. Anyone at the lunch table could do that for them. As a true friend, your deposit of challenging them to stay on the PATH is much more valuable.

Pray for Them: It must please God immensely when we pray for each other. From God's perspective, it's a sign that we get that we are all connected together on the way back to the Garden. Imagine a spider web. The spider creates the web from the center out, slowly and methodically running new silken threads first out from the center and then connecting them by looping new threads all around the web. That's what the Land of OP looks like. We are all interconnected and anchored to the God who made us (the center of the web). When you pray for your friend, the energy in your little area is sent out into the web by way of all those connections.

Give and Receive Critical Feedback: An airplane flying from Minneapolis to Dallas is off course most of the time, yet always ends up in Dallas. Why is that? It's because the pilot is constantly making adjustments based on feedback from the air traffic controllers. They are aware of things the pilot is not seeing, like wind patterns, weather conditions, and other aircraft. Without that feedback, the plane could end up in New Orleans.

Your closest friends and confidants are your own Personal Air Traffic Controllers (PATCs), offering feedback at critical moments.

Critical Feedback:
Thoughts or insights shared in order to identify needed areas of growth and improvement.

Receiving Critical Feedback: Since you are on the PATH, you know that there are things you aren't seeing and, as a result, you can get LOST. You're aware of your NTHs and temptations and so you try to stay on Plank Alert. One of the ways you do that is by asking for critical feedback from your PATCs. Borrowing from the depth of their Trust Fund with you, true friends (as well as parents, trusted adults, and wiser older siblings) can perform this crucial function.

As important as it is to receive critical feedback, it can be difficult to hear and accept. The main hurdle is defensiveness. Critical feedback is saying, "You need to change. You have to do it differently or be different." The strength of your relationship allows those closest to you to say challenging things and speak with honesty about your choices and actions, even if it means risking losing your love and affection as a result. **As long as you are open to the truth, you'll be able to take their feedback to heart and steer yourself back on course.**

TRUE TALES I was a mess during a time in high school. It took the courage of my BFF putting our friendship on the line to save me. She asked me to meet her in the chapel of our high school one day during study hall. Looking back on it now, I recognize that she was giving me crucial critical feedback. It was raw, honest, hard to listen to and very, very important. She struggled through my mess, found me, and directed me back towards the PATH. I thank her to this day.

Giving Critical Feedback: Delivering critical feedback well is an art. As a true friend you will sometimes find yourself in the position of a PATC with a challenging message to share. A few essential steps will ease your discomfort level and the recipient's defensiveness by **framing your feedback in your friend's best interest** and intended to help him remain on the PATH.

1. **Invite Jesus into your yoke:** You are about to enter a challenging conversation. Wouldn't it be great if you recognized that Jesus is right there with you, watching and helping? Ask for the words you need to help your friend hear and understand that you are offering this feedback because you care.
2. **Communicate your sincerity:** Be direct and let your friend know this

is important. Use words you are comfortable with. Here are some examples:

- "Look, I care about you. I've got some thoughts about what's going on."
- "Hey man. Can we talk? Maybe I can help you see this differently."
- "I don't know what all is going on, but I care about you and would really like to talk about what I see happening."

3. **Get permission:** Asking for permission will reduce your friend's defensiveness by giving him some control in the situation. Ask him, "I'd like to share something with you that might be helpful. Would you like to hear it?" If he says yes, then ask: "Would now be a good time?" Follow through wherever the answer leads, setting up a time to talk later if need be. If he says no, then defensiveness is standing in your way. You could say, "If there is a time you want to hear it, let me know." And walk away. The seed was planted.

4. **Present the issue in a questioning way and listen first:** For example, rather than saying, "I don't think you're studying enough," ask him, "How have you been studying for the tests?" Instead of opening with, "You're really bashing your mom all the time these days," open with, "Have you thought of any ways to improve things with your mom?"

5. **Give your feedback:** After listening intently to your friend, share your thoughts or opinions:

   - "I've been concerned. Not turning in your homework assignments is creating a problem for you in Math."
   - "It's been uncomfortable being over at your house lately. Sometimes it seems as if you're pushing your mom's buttons for no reason."

6. **Offer to help problem solve:** "Do you want some help figuring this out?"

Giving critical feedback is a crucial function between close friends and only robust Trust Funds can support it. As with all the skills you'll learn for traveling in the Land of OP, critical feedback will offer you an opportunity to grow your Virtue Quotient. **While giving critical feedback, you will be developing the virtues of tact, empathy, honesty, and even a bit of risk taking. Receiving critical feedback presents an opportunity to increase your resiliency, reflectivity, and humility.**

Like the flight from Minneapolis to Dallas, your journey on the PATH is more successful when you receive solid critical feedback.

Two Roads Diverged

TRUE TALES From that time on, Jesus began to show his disciples that he must go to Jerusalem and suffer greatly from the elders, the chief priests, and the scribes, and be killed and on the third day be raised. Then Peter took him aside and began to rebuke him, "God forbid, Lord! No such thing shall ever happen to you." He turned and said to Peter, "Get behind me, Satan! You are an obstacle to me. You are thinking not as God does, but as human beings do."
Matthew 16:21-23

Jesus knew his True Purpose. He would suffer and he would die and he would rise again in order to show us that following God's will is the PATH. Peter couldn't deal with the truth and tried to convince Jesus that there was another way. He was LOST. Jesus recognized the Emperor at work in Peter and he did not mince words: "Get behind me, Satan."

Your future will bring school changes, address changes, and career changes. On top of those big changes are the more typical changes (hobbies, dating, and school activities) that occur as you make your way through school and beyond. All of these changes move folks in and out of your PATH, resulting in some friendships ending and new ones developing. This can take place naturally over time, with both friends realizing it is happening and gracefully moving on. Other times, though, the break is difficult. You may notice you no longer share the same interests as your friends. You may become uncomfortable with their choices, new friends, or point of view. In these situations, you'll want to have the tools you need to protect yourself and respectfully remove yourself from the relationship. You can use the **L-E-T** method, short for Letting Go:

L **Limit Your Time:** If you determine that a certain friend is having too much negative influence on you, begin by **limiting the time you spend** with her. Instead of spending two nights on the weekend together, just spend one. A good way of limiting your availability is by making other plans. In this way, you can keep to the task of Truth Telling, rather than succumbing to the temptation to tell a lie or to throw up an excuse shield.

E **Expand Your Circle of Friendships:** Think about the various groups of friends you have. The fewer the number, the more influence those friends or groups will have on you. That will leave you with fewer options. On the flip side, **the more friends or groups you have, the less influence any particular group will have on you.** This creates more options.

What could you do to expand your circle of friends?

- Get involved in a new club at school.
- Make good impressions on other classmates by noticing them (those Random Acts of Kindness).
- Set a goal to start up a conversation with three people outside your circle by the end of the month.
- Make deposits in the Trust Fund of a classmate with whom you would like to start a friendship.

Terminate the Relationship: Sometimes it is necessary to end the relationship. When is it time to terminate a relationship? You may have tried talking about the problem by offering critical feedback or you may have tried being a positive influence, but it's not getting any better. **If a relationship is continually tempting you to step off the PATH, it's time to terminate.**

Here's how you might handle the difficult task of termination:

1. Who are your Personal Air Traffic Controllers? Put an X on the continuum representing how willing you are to receive critical feedback from your PATCs.

Unwilling Willing

2. Is there someone you're concerned about who could benefit from your critical feedback? Put an X on the continuum representing your willingness to offer that feedback.

Unwilling Willing

3. Identify any negative influences in your social life. Do you need to:

- Limit your time with someone?
- Expand your friendships?
- Terminate a relationship?

Choose a favorite place and get comfortable.

Begin with the Sign of the Cross. Ask Jesus to be with you during this prayer time.

Talk with Jesus about your two closest friends. You can share:

- Favorite memories
- Characteristics you admire
- Concerns and worries you have

End your prayer by genuinely thanking Jesus for these friends and asking his continued blessing on them.

Close with the Sign of the Cross.

Chapter Twenty-One

Co-Travelers: Mentors

For lack of guidance a people falls;
security lies in many counselors.
Proverbs 11:14

Your true friends will bless your life with devotion and camaraderie, but there is an essential role they cannot fulfill. A mentor (usually someone older and more experienced) can advise and guide you as you travel through the Land of Other People. Your mentor's collection of wisdom and insights will be of great benefit to you. As a fair and impartial observer, your mentor can help **you see your blind spots and look at a situation or person from another angle. Mentors are plank detectors.**

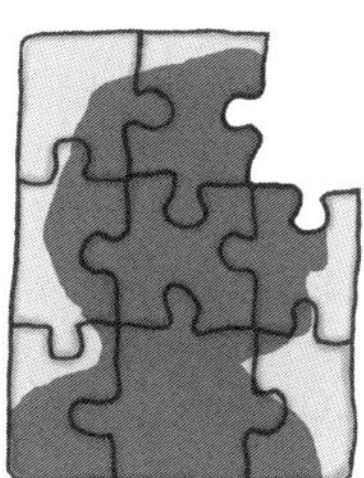

The Land of OP is loaded with unique individuals and each one will need a particular type of mentor. Much like a puzzle piece, the right mentoring type fits your edges. As we take a brief look at each one, be thinking about the older and more experienced people in your life. It's possible that the beginning of a mentoring relationship is already taking place between you and an aunt or uncle, older sibling, teacher, core team member, grandparent, or neighbor.

Mentor as Advisor: An advisor provides an especially dynamic type of advice. The advisor's goal is to help you to be self-reliant and independent, so you will not be told what to do in a given situation. Instead, **his broad suggestions assist you in identifying concrete steps that will move you in the direction you want to go.**

Example 1: After sharing your frustration with how your friends are starting to expect you to share your homework with them because you are 'the smart one,' your mentor says, "Well, as the smart one, what options do you see yourself having?" After hearing you out, he helps you consider those options and come up with some strategies for putting the one you want to follow in place.

Example 2: You've got a part time job babysitting and the parents pay you in cash. You've been keeping the money in a jar on your desk, but lately you've started to suspect that someone is helping himself to it. Your mentor says, "Sounds like you might want to open a bank account." The follow through and responsibility is up to you.

Mentor as Coach: No elite athlete becomes elite without coaching and no one successfully makes it through the Land of OP alone. A PATH coach brings a lifetime of experience, learning, and history to her relationship with you and, because she loves God and you, she wants to see you thrive. She knows what methods work because she's tried most of them and studied the others. She's seen what the other team's (the Emperor) got to offer so she can create a game plan to thwart him.

On top of all that, she knows exactly how to motivate YOU. **Because she's tuned in to your areas of strength (VQ) and weaknesses (NTHs and temptations), your coach is pretty good at individualizing your training.** She is generous with positive feedback—the type that lets you know when you are doing great, steady as you go, and on the mark—and not afraid to offer the critical feedback you need when you are veering off the PATH.

Mentor as Guide: Similar to the coach, but distinctly different, is the guide. He also has great expertise, knowledge, and wisdom to offer you for the PATH. Unlike the coach, however, **the guide's own personal path is what he shares with you.** His playbook is not thick like the coach's because he is an expert only in his distinct area. His knowledge of that area is deep and intense.

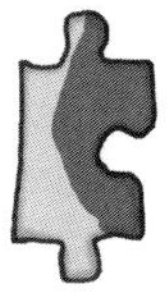

Finding this type of mentor is a rare privilege. You share a common experience of God and find that you are traveling on a similar road through the Land of OP. Perhaps your personalities are complementary or you share a common history of strong experiences that have shaped your lives. It's similar to the relationship between Obiwan Kenobi and Luke Skywalker in the *Star Wars* movies.

Mentor as Friend: Many mentoring relationships take this form. Let's say your mentorship began with a teacher in 6th grade when she was your homeroom teacher. During the rest of grade school, you sometimes stayed after school to help her organize her room and file papers. Those afternoons gave you opportunities to continue talking about what was going on in your life. She was a great listener and helped you PATH your way through a couple of difficult episodes during 7th grade. Over time you learned a lot about her, what it was like when she was in 7th grade, and how she first felt the tug to be a teacher.

This type of day in, day out relationship building with a trusted adult can lead to an awesome, powerful mentoring relationship. In fact, many of the other mentor styles will also take on the style of friendship over time. It is the logical outcome of sharing the PATH together.

If you wish, you can be wiser;
If you are willing to listen, you can learn;
if you pay attention, you can be instructed.
Stand close to the company of the elders;
stay close to whoever is wise.
If you see the intelligent, seek them out;
let your feet wear away their doorsteps!
Sirach 6:32a, 33-36

A Different Breed of Mentor: the Saints As Role Models

Movie Stars. MLB, NBA an NFL Players. Boy Bands and Pop Stars. Olympic Medalists. We buy their T-shirts, shoes, bobble-heads, and jerseys. Their faces are plastered on cereal boxes, magazine covers, and webpages. Their tweets are followed by thousands. Why? Because each of them has become the best in their field and the role model for many who aspire to 'make it.'

This book is about making it in things far more significant than the music industry, Hollywood, and sports. It's about making it in the *important stuff*: finding your God-given purpose and living it out in the Land of OP.

Role Model: a person whose excellence in behavior, example, or success deserves to be imitated. Certainly, no more excellent role models are in this line of work than the saints. They made a commitment to the PATH and then spent their lifetimes building up their VQ, de-planking, reframing, making deposits, and facing and conquering their temptations. Their GPS had one 'to' location: the Garden. Navigating there involved every road and turn that led to God's will.

Modern America can be *anti-Saint* because it can be *anti-PATH*. Our culture focuses on looking out for #1, doing as little as possible but still being successful (say what?), refusing to be inconvenienced or uncomfortable, and getting more stuff. All of these attitudes are opposite of the Grand Design because they all scream "ME!" They Edge God Out by turning all attention and energy to ourselves. Basically, every day offers us apple after apple after apple. We have to learn how to choose not to take a bite and **EGO.**

The saints show us that the PATH is not only possible but that it can make headlines. They show us holiness is big news and downright appealing. During their lifetimes, for example, Pope Saint John Paul II and Blessed Mother Teresa were like lightning rods for newspapers and the television news. Their witness to the world captured us because they spoke directly to our souls, sometimes as if God was speaking, saying, "You, too, can do this." The saints' names and their stories endure. They speak to the true self inside each of us and say, "It's possible to PATH."

The challenge to each of us is to remove the planks from our own eyes when we consider the word 'saint'. We all carry an idea of what a saint is, does, and looks like. Do any of these ring a bell?

- *Boring:* All they do is pray and stuff.
- *Loner:* Didn't they live in caves and cells? I'm a people person.
- *Way too holy:* Seriously? Folded hands and downcast eyes all the time? None for me, thanks.
- *Can't picture it:* Based on the statues, I don't think I'd look good in flowing robes.
- *Freaky:* Weird stuff happened to them. Stigmata? Flying? You've got to be kidding.
- *Way too far outside the norm:* Can you imagine what my friends would say if I acted like that?

The best way to break any stereotype is to get to know someone in the group. Find out about actual individuals rather than make a judgment call based on second-hand information picked up from others. To break the dreaded saint stereotype you've got to get to know a few of them. If that thought inspired you to roll your eyes or think, "That sounds like work," well, both of those reactions are planks that could use a little jiggling. Spending some energy soaking up their stories is, in fact, a better use of your time

than soaking up most of what mainstream media, news, commercials, social networking, music, movies, and cable have to offer you.

You'll need all the guidance and help you can get for the PATH. Why not take advantage of those who have traveled the road ahead of you, creating tracks for you to follow?

A saint exists for every personality type, every passion, and every interest. As role models of virtues, they motivate and inspire us to build up our own VQs by following their example and learning from them.

Just the Beginning

Truth be told, you are just setting out on the PATH. The journey will last your lifetime. You will find yourself crossing paths with all types of co-travelers. If you listen well you will be led to explore places and people you couldn't have imagined. Your mentors will be guideposts for you. They will be sources of guidance, encouragement, affirmation, and challenge. Begin investing time now into building these priceless relationships.

You can give no greater honor or privilege to important adults in your life than to ask them to walk this journey with you. While they may not know it as the PATH, they will understand it is the most important excursion you will ever make.

1. Make a list of the important adults in your life. Indicate which type of mentor each one has the potential of becoming for you.

2. Make a list of the children who are important to you. Then indicate which type of mentor you could potentially become for each of them.

The saints in heaven are *always* praying. Because of this, their prayers for us can be even more powerful than our own. Choose a saint (your Confirmation saint, a personal favorite or one you learned about on page 11). Identify one quality of this saint that you admire and hope to increase in yourself. Then begin your prayer.

Pray the sign of the cross and ask Jesus to guide you in praying with your chosen saint.

On the PATH

Greet your saint and ask him or her to be with you during this time of prayer.

Talk to him or her about the quality you have selected. Explain why you want to increase it and how it will help you keep on the PATH.

Ask him or her to pray for you and be a mentor to you.

Thank your saint for his or her prayers and guidance.

Close with the Sign of the Cross.

Chapter Twenty-Two

Stormy Weather

When traveling cross-country, it's wise to check on the weather forecast. If there's heavy snow expected in the mountains, you might put off leaving until it passes. If your smart phone indicates a severe line of thunderstorms ahead, you may try to reroute in order to avoid the worst of it. However, sometimes your schedule is so tight you can't detour around bad weather. You have to plow straight ahead and use your best driving skills to make it safely through the storm.

In recent years, technology has allowed us to witness the tremendous energy of tornadoes from the safety of our couches. We've watched them develop and descend, viewed them from the cameras of tornado chasers, and seen the devastating vacuum cleaner effect of their power.

A person or group operating Below the Line or in the midst of a Thought Circle can produce **a social Tornado, an invisible and destructive force of negativity with the potential to turn nasty and sinful.** Like a natural tornado, a social Tornado gets its power from the environment around it. If the social environment is stable, a Tornado cannot develop. But if the environment is teeming with boredom, anger, or discontent, conditions are ripe for a social Tornado to develop. It is totally possible that an otherwise innocent Above the Line bystander can be drawn into a Tornado and BTL if he is not 'watching the weather' and planning accordingly.

As people of the PATH, it is our duty to avoid these social Tornadoes, de-energize them if possible, and resist the temptation to start them ourselves. As the Catechism says (Catholic Church, 2302), **one of our tasks as members of the Mystical Body is to "safeguard peace."** We are to be peacemakers, bridge builders, and conflict resolvers because we know that the Grand Design has us moving towards God and the Kingdom together. We can only do this when we work to create and maintain peace among the travelers in the Land of OP.

How Tornadoes Are Formed

Our communication with other people is often an attempt to influence them, gain agreement, or win support for our views. If our views are negative, a Tornado can be spawned and draw in unsuspecting victims. As it grows more and more intense, a Tornado tends to dominate the culture of the group.

What causes this to happen? A common response to someone complaining is to add our own complaining, even if it is a complaint about something else. In some relationships it becomes almost like an automatic reflex. This response may come from our need to connect, belong, or be accepted. Or it may be that we need to battle the EE's temptation to use a blame thrower, which allows us to fall BTL or into a Thought Circle. Either way, he's got us straying away from the PATH.

The conversation between Jake and Tim has taken on the nature of a spewing contest. Each participant upchucks negative energy on to the other. From your perspective on the PATH, you can see exactly what is going on here. It's a Tornado. Time to reroute.

The Three Levels of Emergency Awareness

Tornado Watch: At Level One we recognize that circumstances and situations are ripe for the creation of a Tornado. My students have consistently pinpointed the same primary condition: *no teachers or parents are in sight.* Locker rooms, hallways, sleepovers, small group work, lunch tables, school bathrooms, Twitter, texting, and during gym class when there's lots of empty, open space are all examples of adult-free zones.

Tornado Warning: At Level Two the first complaint or negative comment has been thrown to the group. Almost always this comment is made about someone who is not present in the group. We've all heard or used phrases like "What is *she* doing talking to *him*" or "Mrs. Moffit's wearing that lame outfit again. She seriously needs a wardrobe makeover."

Tornado Touchdown: Level Three is in progress once someone in the group responds by jumping in to agree with that complaint or adding his own. Quickly the conversation degenerates into a ping-pong match of complaints: negative comment-complaint-evil words-complaint, and so on. This happens rapidly, often within 30 seconds or less.

Tornado Watch	Tornado Warning	Tornado Touchdown
Conditions are right for tornadoes	Funnel cloud sighted	Tornado has pulled in others
Adult-free Zone After a loss Hallways Social media Gym class Bathrooms Lunch tables Small group work Sleepovers Practice	Negative comment made about something or someone who is absent	Be on the look out for the following features: Furtive glances Heads close together Whispering Escalating volume Sarcasm Mocking Imitating

Responding to Tornadoes

We might like to carry a magic wand to wave over Tornado starters to get them to change. Unfortunately, such magic wands have not yet been invented. While you can't change folks in the Land of OP, the following techniques will help you recognize, avoid, and do your part to dismantle the Tornadoes that cross your PATH.

1. Be on Watch: Most tornadoes in the U.S. occur in the central states in an area referred to as Tornado Alley. I happen to live there. When a Tornado Watch is issued, we don't change our plans, but we do watch for storm clouds and wind shifts. You can do the same with social Tornadoes. Pay attention to where Tornadoes tend to occur in your school and among your friends. Watch for the signs and steer clear if you can.

2. Name It: If you find yourself walking into a Tornado or unable to avoid its development, tell yourself, "Uh oh, sounds like there's a Tornado going on here." The Tornado will be front and center in your mind, allowing you to gather your energies for the work of staying out of it.

3. Listen with Shields Up: Learn the difference between listening to what someone is saying and taking what they are saying to heart. As soon as you take what they are saying to heart, you will go where they are. It is important that you learn to listen without agreeing.

4. Respond by Saying, "I hear you": Not all Tornado starters are out to wreak havoc. We all have a bad day, sit through a boring class, receive a poor grade, or find ourselves the target of someone's unkind remark. Needing to talk about it is natural. Being able to comfort someone who is having a bad day is a real gift. Sometimes a Tornado will dissipate if the starter feels like she was heard and understood. By saying, "I hear you," you acknowledge her experience without adding more negative energy to the Tornado. This simple strategy also works when you innocently walk into a Tornado already in full swing. Back to our cartoon, previously in progress. . .

Jake and Tim both look at Brian as if to say, "It's your turn to rip on somebody." Brian feels the pressure and anticipates the social punishment that would come his way if he doesn't play along. What he would really like to share with his buddies is his good news: "Hey, guys, I've got a date for the dance Saturday night." But he knows that doing so will only direct Tim and Jake's wrath towards him.

Instead, Brian gives a response that doesn't feed the negative energy, but lets both Jake and Tim know he gets what they're going through. He observes the Tornado, but is not damaged by it. He recognizes his friends' situation but is neither affected by it nor victimizes others. He steers clear of the Emperor's maneuverings.

5. Stay or Go: While "I hear you" is a very effective response to a Tornado, sometimes a Tornado's energy is so great that it doesn't respond to the strategy, even if you repeat it again. In this type of situation you have two choices: walk away or speak up.

Walk Away: A situation may be well outside your comfort zone or beyond your abilities. Perhaps your courage and fortitude are not strong enough to directly challenge a full-blown Tornado. In these situations, the best you can do is to get up and walk away from the event.

Should you choose to remain, you become associated with the group of Tornado makers in the mind of others. Whether or not you participated, you were present. Over time you will develop the reputation of someone who rips on others. It's the way the Land of OP works. We get there together, wherever 'there' happens to be.

Speak Up: As mentioned above, not everyone on the PATH is ready or called to take this role, but there are those who have been given outgoing personalities and clarity of speech. When coupled with a VQ strong in the virtues of justice, courage, and confidence, your feelings of discomfort and agitation in the presence of a Tornado may well be the whisper of the Holy Spirit inviting you to "safeguard peace" by stepping inside a Tornado and challenging it. Check out Paul's first letter to the Corinthians, 12:24-26:

God has so constructed the body as to give greater honor
to a part that is without it,
so that there may be no division in the body,
but that the parts may have the same concern for one another.
If one part suffers, all the parts suffer with it;
if one part is honored, all the parts share its joy.

Remember how most Tornadoes rip on someone who is not present? Paul is direct and insistent in his teaching about how we are to care for each other in this kind of situation. The member lacking honor is missing in action. That member's reputation is suffering. As members of One Body and observers of a cruel Tornado, Paul tells us that *we should all suffer* because one of us is being ridiculed, mocked, demeaned, and dishonored.

If it is your gift to step in, Paul is telling you that you most likely should.

1. In your experience, what situations most often produce social Tornadoes? Consider school, extra-curricular activities, weekend settings, and social media outlets.

2. Where do you find yourself starting Tornadoes?

Start with the Sign of the Cross.

Ask Jesus to help you be humble and honest during this prayer time.

Recall a Tornado you were a part of. Describe it to Jesus, focusing on your role in it and what you wish you had done differently.

Pray for the person who was the most damaged by that Tornado and offer an Act of Contrition.

Rest with Jesus for a while. Feel his mercy and confidence in your ability to steer clear of Tornadoes in the future.

End with the Sign of the Cross.

Chapter Twenty-Three

Hits

Do not fear: I am with you; do not be anxious: I am your God.
I will strengthen you, I will help you, I will uphold you.
Isaiah 41:10

So, here you are out on the wide-open roads of the PATH. You've been absorbed in thought about the various strategies and skills you've learned. A few names have come to mind when you think about finding a mentor. You've managed to sidestep a Tornado or two, though you haven't quite spoken up yet. All in all, you feel like you're beginning to get the hang of it. And then, *bam!* It happens. You take a Hit.

- A friend lets one of your secrets slip and now everyone knows.
- A teacher corrects you pretty fiercely in front of the whole class.
- Somebody makes a negative comment about your hair, shoes, or lunch.
- You're cut from the team.

Hits are unexpected random negative events that trigger a response or reaction. Like the potholes we encounter along the road, Hits have the potential of knocking us off the PATH. Sometimes we can swerve to avoid them; more often than not, though, we hit them at full speed.

The Frame teaches that how you think about a Hit will produce your feelings which will lead to your actions and ultimately an outcome (Think-Feel-Do-Get). Unfortunately, those feelings are usually pretty negative and lead to costly reactions.

Feelings From Hits		Reactions To Hits	
Angry	Unappreciated	Judging others	Seeking revenge
Depressed	Powerless	Withdrawing	Swearing
Embarassed	Overwhelmed	Being apathetic	Fighting verbally or physically
Worried	Stupid	Giving up	Crying
Humiliated	Defeated	Being sarcastic	Spreading gossip
Hurt	Frustrated	Sulking	

You'll experience Hits for the rest of your days on earth. With this many folks traveling through the Land of OP—some on the PATH, some figuring out how the PATH works, many who are LOST—Hits are just a product of the terrain. If you wake up every day knowing that today likely has a Hit or two in store for you, then you are framing Hits with an "It's just my turn" thought rather than an "It's just not fair" thought.

Handling Hits: LOST Style

As you would expect, being on the PATH or LOST has an enormous influence on how a person deals with a Hit. As soon as someone who is LOST experiences a Hit she REACTs. The Frame chain snaps into place before she can exert any control over the process. The Hit happens, the negative feeling sets in, the rude or angry comeback (a cut down, a shove, a complaint, an accusation, a punch, a whine) comes out, and the consequences follow. *Bam! Bam! Bam!*

Other common reactions to a Hit include:

- Making rash judgments about others
- Yelling, cussing
- Getting quiet; going inside yourself
- Giving up
- Sarcasm
- Spreading gossip
- Employing blamethrowers and excuse shields
- Lashing out at innocent bystanders

Handling Hits: PATH Style

It's a whole different ball game when you are dedicated to the PATH. You are working hard to see how every single moment and interaction can help you move closer to your True Purpose and further along the road. How can this Hit help you to love God more fiercely? How can you treat this person well in God's name? Remember Fr. Caussade's Sacrament of the Present Moment?

A Hit is one of the ultimate tests of your willingness to meet God in the Upper Left Corner of the Frame and say, "This stinks! Show me how to find You in this. Show me how to be like You here and now."

Reread page 110 if you've forgotten what the Sacrament of the Present Moment is!

The most important tool a person of the PATH can bring to a Hit is something we spoke about back in the chapter titled *Confronting NTHs and Temptations: Tools for In the Moment.* It's mastering the Art of the Stop.

You have probably noticed that many drivers do not make a full and complete stop at a stop sign. They kind of roll through it, giving a quick glance left and right to check for cross traffic.

Great wisdom (Hey! That's a virtue!) is attainable if you come to a complete and full STOP when you suffer a Hit. Pressing the pause button gives you the time you need to regroup. Use that time to get yourself to the ULC and shout to God, "Get over here now!" Yes, you should feel comfortable speaking to God this way. This is the Real Deal and God is all about the Real Deal. It's the truth about what's going on.

Leaning on God helps you to see from another perspective. It's the power of the Holy Spirit—the advocate Jesus sent as our supporter and backer—that helps you develop the virtues of humility, curiosity, and determination as you dig deeper into the Real Deal that is taking place during a Hit. Isn't that awesome! *This* is who Jesus sent us at Pentecost.

The Advocate, the Holy Spirit that the Father will send in my name—He will teach you everything and remind you of all that I told you.
–John 14:26

The following diagram illustrates the difference between how people of the PATH and those who are LOST encounter Hits.

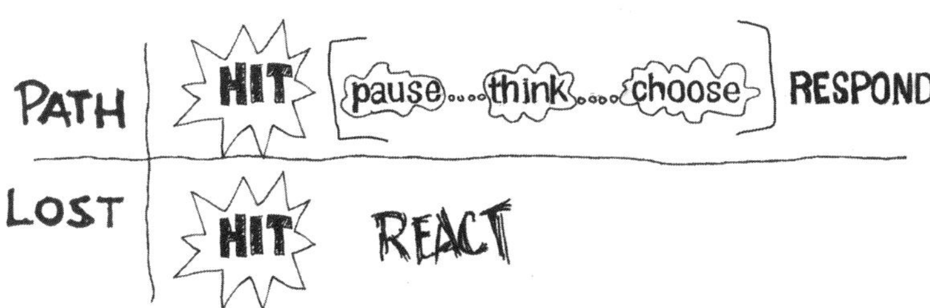

Perspective

Why do we react so quickly and so strongly to Hits? Often there's a plank in the way and we are having a tough time seeing from the perspective of the person delivering the Hit. Let's look at three examples of Hits and see how the kids' perspectives might be different from the adults' perspectives.

Hit 1: A student walks into class after the bell and the teacher says, "You're late."
The *student* sees this as an attack in public.
The *teacher* sees it as simply informing the student of being unacceptably tardy unless the student has a valid excuse.

Hit 2: A player runs the wrong play during a basketball game and is taken out by the coach.
The *player* sees this as humiliation in front of a crowd.
The *coach* sees it as wanting to explain to a confused player how to run the play correctly.

Hit 3: A girl is about to leave for a dance in a tank top when her mother says, "Go back upstairs and take that off."
The *daughter* sees her mother as overprotecting and a control freak.
The *mother* is concerned about how her daughter might be judged by others if she's wearing a revealing tank top.

What's the moral of these stories? **When you are in the ULC, ask for the willingness to see from a perspective other than your own.** It's a big Land of OP. What might you learn about yourself or the other person in this moment? Is there some NTH that this Hit is suggesting you confront? Is this Hit an opportunity for you to strengthen a specific virtue? Or, perhaps this difficult interaction, if done right, will help the other person grow a virtue.

A Hit offers you an immense amount of power:

- The power to control your own thoughts and feelings.
- The power to become a caretaker of peace.
- The power to look more like the Maker every day.

Frame a hit that way and you'll find purpose and value in it.

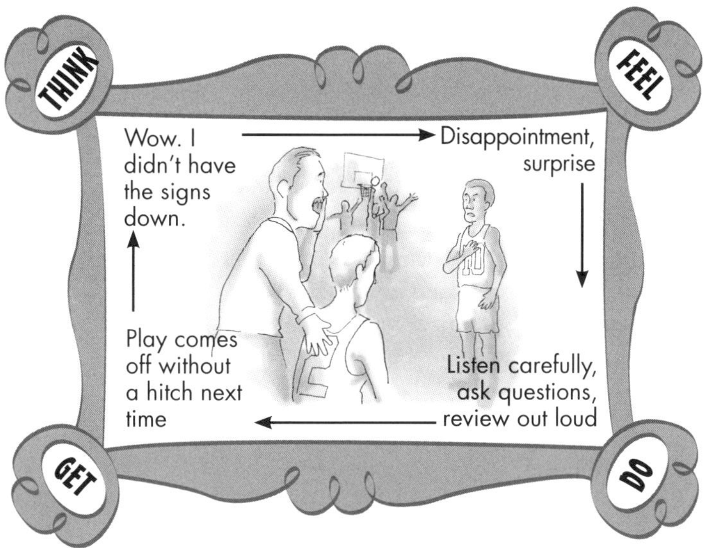

The Bigger Question

"Why should I do all the work and be an upright guy? What if the other guy thinks I'm a loser or a push over, and walks all over me?"

In 2011, the movie *Captain America* took theaters around the world by storm. It grossed over $369,000,000 and that was before it was released on DVD and to Netflix. Why was this comic-book-made-movie a blockbuster? Because the underdog, straight up guy was able to save the day, precisely because he was a straight up guy.

Before Captain America, we had Luke Skywalker, Indiana Jones, and Spiderman. We watched them in action and were caught up in their heroism, their bravery, their determination to fight evil, their ability to withstand pain, and their willingness to make the ultimate sacrifice in the name of good, if it came to that.

Now reread that last paragraph, but insert the name of Jesus into it. (As always, I will wait.) **He is the example on which all our Superheroes are built.** He calls us to be his sidekicks in real life, not just in a fantasy story or digital dream. He challenges each of us to say "Yes" to working with him for the cause of good, even in the difficult times. And Hits are certainly the difficult times.

We know that Jesus is God who came to earth to show us how to 'do human' and do it right. If you've paid attention to his story, you know that being *like* him will involve some suffering and hardship. Following him asks you to choose the harder path when you face struggles and Hits. **Following him means you choose to respond rather than react.** At no time ever are you saying you like to suffer when you choose the PATH. What you are saying is, "I want to be like him because he is the way of truth that leads to life."

When it comes to Hits, this means you'll do what it takes to master yourself by learning how to push the pause button. You'll do what it takes to remember and live out the second part of your True Purpose: to be good to others in God's name.

When you come to serve the Lord,
prepare yourself for trials.
Be sincere of heart and steadfast,
and do not be impetuous in time of adversity.
Cling to him, do not leave him,
that you may prosper in your last days.
Accept whatever happens to you;
in periods of humiliation be patient.
For in fire gold is tested,
and the chosen, in the crucible of humiliation.
Trust in God, and he will help you;
make your ways straight and hope in him.
Sirach 2:1-6

1. Recall a time when your reaction to a Hit made the situation worse.

2. How would the results of this situation have been different if you had pressed the pause button and invited Jesus to the ULC before responding?

Pray the Sign of the Cross and meet Jesus in the ULC.

On a piece of paper draw a large cross to fill the page.

Bring to mind a difficult Hit you have taken recently. Use one word to identify it and write the word on the crossbeam.

In the area below the crossbeam write and complete this sentence: "It's hard for me to follow you in difficult times because...."

In the area above the crossbeam write and complete this sentence: "When it comes to handling Hits in the future, I hope to...."

Offer a spontaneous prayer thanking Jesus for showing you how to carry a cross with dignity. Ask him to give you the strength to create win-win results out of conflicts.

Close with the Sign of the Cross.

Chapter Twenty-Four

Road Rage

As long as we're dealing with challenging topics like Hits, let's look at another tough one: dealing with conflicts while PATHing.

Conflicts are fights, disagreements, clashes, sometimes downright battles, and they are another reality in the Land of Other People. **Learning to approach conflicts from the ULC is a responsibility we share as members of The Body and as the "safeguards of peace."**

Live in a manner worthy of the call you have received,
with all humility and gentleness, with patience,
bearing with one another through love,
striving to preserve the unity of the spirit
through the bond of peace.
Ephesians 4:1-3

The LOST style of approaching conflicts is toe-to-toe. Consider the sport of boxing: two boxers stand toe-to-toe in a tight space and take swings at each other. If you want to win, you've got to knock the other guy out. It's pretty clear that this isn't what Jesus had in mind when he showed us how to do human the right way.

The problem with the LOST style is how the Frame of the conflict begins. In the ULC, thoughts might sound something like this illustration:

Noticing a pattern? Each of these thoughts finds our LOST traveler setting up a win-lose scenario. Somebody is right and somebody is wrong. Someone is going to win and someone is going to lose. And you know who she think is going to come out on the winning side!

No peace. No unity. No virtues.

The PATH approach to conflicts is win-win. You look for benefit for both yourself and the other person. No one loses because the resolution is positive for both of you. **The win-win approach is built on a rock solid Jesus-principle and core teaching of Christianity: love your neighbor.** Throughout this book we've said the same thing in a different way: treat others well in God's name.

Love Who?

In Luke's Gospel (6:32-33, 35-36), Jesus challenged the crowd (and every human being who will eventually read the Bible) with the following questions and instruction:

> *If you love those who love you, what credit is that to you?*
> *Even sinners love those who love them.*
> *If you do good to those who do good to you, what credit is that to you?*
> *Even sinners do the same.*
> *But rather, love your enemies and do good to them...*
> *then your reward will be great and you will be children of the Most High,*
> *for He Himself is kind to the ungrateful and the wicked.*
> *Be merciful, just as your Father is merciful.*

What does all this mean? It's saying that anyone can be nice to people they like. The real test is to be nice to those you can't stand. When you are in the middle of a conflict, you sometimes find yourself dangerously close to 'can't standing.'

The mandate to love our neighbor is a cornerstone of being a Christian and we start hearing about it early on. But it's darn difficult to live out. In fact, if you took an anonymous poll of those in your grade and asked them if they make a real effort to be nice to people they can't stand, well, let's just say the poll would be skewed toward the 'no' answer. **The fact is, we know what we are supposed to do. We just don't know how to do it.** What we need are some solid thinking strategies and a few concrete actions to put into practice. We need to learn skills for loving our enemies, not just a quote from the Bible.

Thinking Strategies: Pause, De-Plank, and Be Pure of Heart

Pause and De-plank: It's Upper Left Corner time. You know and have begun practicing this skill. When the conflict begins, get yourself to ULC as soon as possible. Train yourself to invite Jesus into the mix to help you restructure your thinking.

It will take some practice to establish this skill because it involves breaking an old habit (reacting). Try these strategies:

- If you are a *visual learner,* bring a stop sign to mind.
- If you *learn best by doing,* pace a little or step from foot to foot while thinking a simple phrase like, "See the big picture!" or "What don't I know?"
- If you *need to hear* it to learn it, go with direct verbal communication. Say out loud, "JC, ULC now!"

When you make the effort to de-plank you are practicing the virtue of humility. **You are reframing the situation by admitting that the world doesn't revolve around you alone.** Maybe this other person has a valid point or something you need to hear. What do you feel, do, and get when you think about a conflict this way in the ULC?

Be Pure of Heart: This is one of the Beatitudes, but what does it mean? It means that your heart and mind are in sync with God's Will. **When your heart is pure, it allows you to see people as God sees them: completely and totally loved, just as you are completely and totally loved.** Yes, this is a tall order. It's asking you to empty out your anger and your need to be right and replace them with the thought that, "Hey, God loves this guy, too."

How can you purify your heart? Try these:

- Take three deep breaths and think "Jesus in" on the inhales and "Anger out" on the exhales.
- Try repeating, "Not mine, but yours." You'll be asking God to override your thoughts with holy thoughts.
- Repeat this phrase to yourself: "You love him, too."

If some of these strategies make you feel awkward or sound far-fetched, remember this: it's the human way to question ideas that are new to us. Some of the coolest outcomes came from questioning:

- Do you think we could fly?
- How do we know the world is flat?
- What do you think it's like on the moon?
- Do you think we could make a phone without a cord?

Questioning what is possible is built into the human spirit and it inspires us to explore, try, and succeed. Ask yourself: "Can I figure out how to see her as loved by God, even though right now I am really peeved with her?" If you reach out for God's assistance, the Spirit who lives inside you will help you try to, and succeed in, loving your enemy.

Once your head and heart are in the right place, you'll be ready to enter into a constructive discussion. In order to help that discussion move along smoothly, you'll need to use the next series of skills.

Concrete Actions: Listening and Talking

At the heart of conflicts are misunderstandings caused by poor communication. To resolve conflicts, we need to clear up the misunderstandings. To clear up misunderstandings, we need to communicate effectively.

Listening: Begin reducing a misunderstanding by *listening to understand* rather than *listening to plan.* What's the difference?

When we *listen to plan* we are listening to judge or find faults and shortcomings in the speaker so we can use them as ammunition the next time we speak. Or, we are using the listening time as an opportunity to plan our comeback, rather than to hear what is being said. These are habits we fall back on if we are not on high alert and self-aware. They are examples of navel-gazing: all attention is on ourselves and making sure we get the next blow in.

Listening to understand means our focus is on the other guy, and it includes:

- Listening for the content (what their actual words mean).
- Listening for feelings (you'll see this in body language and hear it in tone of voice).
- Checking your work (saying back in paraphrase form what you heard or saw).

The goal of this method is to guarantee you understand the other person correctly and that you have not jumped to conclusions or attached other meanings to verbal or non-verbal messages. When you check your work, including both content and feeling, and it is accurate, the speaker knows that she is understood. If it is inaccurate, she can correct the inaccuracy until understanding is reached.

Notice how the outcome of Option 1 on the next page is a bigger mess, while Option 2 opened the door to further discussion. It reduced negative energy and allowed time to de-plank and get a handle on the other person's perspective. Because he felt understood, Dad was more willing to listen. All of this can result in an opportunity to *love your neighbor.*

Talking: You've put in the effort to listen well and verify that you understand what is being communicated to you. Now it's your turn to speak. By sticking to a few guidelines you'll keep the negative energy at bay and the listener's defensiveness down.

1. *The Power of I:* One thing that is guaranteed to make a conflict worse is when people feel blamed or accused. The primary way this occurs is when the speaker makes 'You' statements. 'You' statements usually begin with the word 'you' and tend to point the finger at the other person, whether directly or indirectly.

Where are you now? The original problem still exists and bigger ones have been created. You are grounded and your relationship with your dad is even more strained. You've taken a definite wrong turn off the PATH. **The mess has gotten messier.**

Where are you now? You de-planked by listening to and understanding your dad's perspective. You took responsibility for coming home late and apologized for the worry you created. Because he was heard, he is more open to listening to you. **The chances of cleaning up this messy conflict are now excellent.**

It's easy to avoid blaming and accusing by switching pronouns and employing the word 'I.' An 'I' statement takes the focus off of what we think the other person has done to us and redirects our talking towards identifying our own feelings and content. Talk about yourself (the only facts you can be sure of), not the other person. To give an 'I' statement real power, add what might help fix the problem.

"YOU" STATEMENTS	"I" STATEMENTS
"You make me angry when you're not home on time."	"I worry when you're not home on time. A phone call would have really helped."
"You never help with the dishes."	"It just feels unfair to me when I'm stuck doing the dishes by myself. Will you grab a towel, please?"
"You never listen to me."	"I'm feeling ignored, like I'm not being listened to. I'll say it again more clearly."
"You always decide what we're going to be doing."	"The decision was made without my input so I feel left out! Let's look at the options together."

2. *Avoid the Comeback Catastrophes:* The following responses are sure to keep you in a toe-to-toe conflict, increase negativity, and drive you farther off the PATH, back towards navel-gazing and a win-lose mentality. Each of us tends to have a few old standby comebacks that we rely on. Can you identify yours? They are NTHs that the Emperor has designed just for you.

The Historian:
"I remember six years ago when you said..."

The Judge:
"You're dead wrong for saying that; thinking that; feeling that."

The Shrink:
"Your problem is that you take things too personally. You're paranoid. You make things up in your head."

The Know It All:
"Let me tell you what you have to do. When I was your age this is what I did."

The Lawyer:
"That's not what I said. Maybe that's what you thought you heard but it's not what I meant. I can prove it. I have witnesses."

The Drill Sergeant:
"Stand right there and don't move when I'm talking to you!"

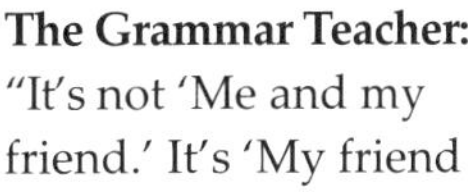

The Mind Reader:
"Oh, I know what you're thinking. I know what you're going to say next."

The Grammar Teacher:
"It's not 'Me and my friend.' It's 'My friend and I'."

The Apathetic:
"Whatever! I don't care."

Resolving the Conflict: Getting There Together

It's true that the win-lose approach is the preferred choice of many people, many societies, and many countries. For them, winning is valued more than peace, unity, and mutual respect. That being said, **the way it is doesn't mean that is how it should be.** As people of the PATH, we are called to something much greater than winning; we are called to getting back to the Garden, together.

For that reason, sometimes you have to be brave (virtue = courage) and take the first step towards loving your neighbor through conflict resolution. Extending an invitation to talk and listen may catch the other person off guard, and they may test your good will and try to push your buttons to see if you are for real. But if you practice patience and tenacity (even more virtues), you will cultivate and create trust over time.

All sorts of signs help keep road traffic flowing safely and smoothly. Sometimes we have to yield. Sometimes we merge. Sometimes our lane is given the right of way. Sometimes we have to make a U-turn. Because we all understand what the signs mean, we trust each other on the roads.

Working through conflict is similar. Sometimes I may find that I was in the wrong and so I will yield to your correction. Sometimes we both have a bit of the truth, so we merge our perspectives together and create a better big picture. Sometimes I am actually right to begin with, you see this, and apologize. And sometimes I am completely off base, have to stop in my tracks, and backtrack to get on the PATH again.

The Jesus way through conflict turns many of the lessons we learn out on the streets of our culture and on the nightly news upside down and inside out. His message is something like this: instead of going to battle, put down your shield and lay down your sword. Remove the threat you are to the other guy by being open to listening, understanding, and even changing something within yourself if it's needed.

Live in a manner worthy of the call you have received,
with all humility and gentleness, with patience,
bearing with one another through love,
striving to preserve the unity of the spirit
through the bond of peace.
Ephesians 4:1-3

1. On the line below, mark an X representing where you tend to fall when involved in a conflict.

Win/Lose | | | | | • | | | | | • | | | | | • | | | | | • | | | | | • Win/Win

2. Identify two Talking or Listening strategies you will work on in order to move toward win/win on the continuum.

Begin with the Sign of the Cross.

Ask Jesus to be in the ULC and help you jiggle a plank during this prayer time.

Bring to mind a relationship in your life that suffers from conflict.

Visualize the person in this difficult relationship. See him or her clearly in a peaceful setting. If negativity tries to enter your thoughts, say, "Not now" and put it in the Parking Lot.

Maintain this peaceful visual as you inhale saying "Jesus in" and exhale saying "Anger out."

After a few moments, offer a spontaneous prayer or a few Hail Marys for this relationship.

End with the Sign of the Cross.

Chapter Twenty-Five

It's Habit Forming

In 6th grade I decided I wanted to play the guitar. I had daydreams of hearing myself on the radio playing the songs I wrote while Americans everywhere sang along. Yeah, I dreamed big! I got a guitar that Christmas and started taking lessons.

That first year was beastly. Lessons consisted in learning to read music and hitting one string at a time with a pick. Trying to play chords was miserable. My fingertips turned bright red from repeatedly pressing flesh into metal. Many a day I spent practicing the same simple skill over and over, making the same mistake over and over. When I didn't bother to practice, my teacher always knew and pointed it out. I couldn't fake hard work. Frustration built up. I just wanted to PLAY! I wanted to be on the radio! I didn't know it was going to take so much effort!

Maybe you are a dancer or a soccer player. Perhaps writing or the theater is your thing. You may have a reputation as the most excellent video game player at your lunch table.

Whatever your thing, it's your thing because you love it, pursue it, and work hard at it. You put in the time because the outcome is worth it to you. When you can't sink a basket for your life, when your avatar gives it up in the first level, or when you strain a muscle trying to learn a new position, you still have your eyes on the goal. The pain, frustration, and setbacks are worth it because, even on the worst day, you are determined to advance towards the prize. Rather than give up, you choose to rest up, heal up, and build up in order to overcome the obstacle next time.

Becoming excellent at something takes time and dedication. Precious few folks come to earth with an innate gift of excellence in anything. We learn how to walk, talk, eat, pick things up, kick a ball, hold our tongue, clean our room, take a good selfie, be a friend, use a smartphone, diagram a sentence, change a tire, and program a remote. Ultimately, everything is learned and success is built on skills mastered. You've got to dribble to play soccer, conjugate verbs to speak Spanish, and know your chords if you ever hope to be on the radio.

It is no different on the PATH. Realize from the beginning that **this is an anti-Google adventure.** Like learning to dribble, conjugate, and chord, you should expect that PATH skill building will be a gradual process. Getting in the yoke is an acquired habit. Reviewing your videos takes time. Developing an intimate friendship with Jesus is a demanding commitment. The ability to de-plank develops with self-awareness and practice. Increasing your VQ results from repetition and conquering your temptations is a daily choice. So set yourself up to succeed by framing the journey correctly. Go to the ULC, flag down Jesus, and say, "Let's go. I'm in it for the long haul."

Your successful journey depends on habits of the Inside, your dedication to mastering them, and your decision to live in God. On the worst day, when you feel as if grace has evaporated and the EE took over your brain, you must still have your eyes on the goal. The struggles, frustration, and setbacks will be worth it if you are determined to advance towards the Garden.

**The skills of the PATH are within your grasp.
First you learn. Then you practice.
Success follows.**

TRUE TALES Eventually, I rounded the corner with my guitar lessons and I could play. My nemesis-turned-best friend and I spent long nights writing songs together. We spent weekend nights at coffee houses playing for an audience. Over time, I was guided to use my passion for God's purposes, though I didn't realize it 'in the moment.' I started playing at school masses, youth group masses, and campus ministry masses in college. Fast-forward: for the last twenty-five years I have made a living using my guitar as a teacher and musician in Catholic schools. It's not the radio, but God had other plans. Pursuing them has been win-win.

Remember, it is your very nature to live in God and this means it is your very nature to be holy. While knitting you into being, God put passions and gifts on your heart, and with your permission God will guide you to use them for holy purposes. Whether you dream of a future as a lawyer or a teacher, a video game designer or an engineer, God will use those passions and gifts **to bless this world by revealing Himself to the rest of us through the potential that is woven into you.**

Say "Yes" to your own potential. Choose the PATH and trust in God's unending devotion to you. Set your GPS to the Garden, get in the yoke with Jesus, and allow the Holy Spirit to lead you on the only journey that truly matters.

Glossary

Above the Line (ATL): when our thinking skills and thought patterns serve us well and bring out the best in us. (77)

After the Fact (ATF): opting to de-plank deeply entrenched NTHs by incorporating regular reflection and step-by-step action plans into our daily lives. (97)

Awareness: our primary defense for identifying and eradicating planks, Negative Thinking Habits, temptations, and Thought Circles. (76, 87)

Baptism: God's sign given to help us return to the Garden; through human things (water, oil, and fire) God gifts us with all we need to pursue our true purpose: grace, the Holy Spirit, removal of original sin, and a community of faith. (106)

Below the Line (BTL): when our thoughts and thinking patterns give rise to pessimism and negativity, reinforce planks, and expose us to manipulation by the Evil Emperor. (77)

Big Shift, The: an explosion of brain development which takes place over a decade of time, normally from early teens through early twenties; characterized by rapid brain growth and the acquisition of executive cognitive skills. (31)

Blame Thrower: a metaphor for our tendency to blame others and avoid personal responsibility. (30)

Cardinal Virtues: four central moral virtues of the Catholic faith: prudence, fortitude, justice, and temperance. (23)

Concupiscence: the tendency toward sin by Edging God Out that is a part of fallen human nature. (107)

Covenant: a bond between two parties with both parties agreeing to certain responsibilities. (118)

Critical Feedback: thoughts or insights shared to assist another in staying on the PATH by identifying areas needing growth and improvement. (127)

De-planking: the act of defusing attitudes, beliefs, or ways of thinking that sabotage our ability to understand a person or situation with clarity. (54-55)

Deposit: a positive contribution to a trust fund. (116-119)

Easing Up: a technique for lowering our conviction of a Negative Thinking Habit. (98)

Edge God Out (EGO): choosing to live apart from God rather than in God; the primary goal of the Evil Emperor; the basis of all sin and evil. (93)

Evil Emperor: title used to personify the presence and reality of evil in our world and lives. (69)

Examen (see also Review Your Videos): a spiritual exercise created by St. Ignatius Loyola to assist seekers in pursuing the will of God. (100)

Excuse Shield: a metaphor for using excuses to deflect personal responsibility. (30)

Fall, The: the first humans' decision to attempt living outside their nature by living apart from God; wanting to be separate yet like God rather than live in God. (63, 65)

Fallen Angel: creatures who profoundly and irreversibly deny their fundamental nature as made in God. (64)

Fess up: acknowledging that we do not understand a situation either completely or with clarity; the first step in de-planking. (56)

Fortitude: strength and courage to do what needs to be done in the face of obstacles. (24)

Frame, The: the Think-Feel-Do-Get metaphor that can be applied to all situations and circumstances and thereby enable an individual to remain on the PATH. (33-34)

Free Will: the gift of choice and self-direction given to humans by God so that we may freely seek Him; the power we have to choose to PATH or to be LOST. (18)

Fullness of Time: when God entered the world in flesh and blood as Jesus. (66)

Fundamental Nature: a person or object's basic, truest purpose as defined by its inventor. (2)

Garden, The: eternal life with God; heaven. (63-65)

Grace: the perpetual and undeserved gift of God's presence in all creation; the gift by which our efforts to return to the Garden are sustained and fortified. (73, 105)

Grand Design: God's will for all of creation which leads to True Happiness. (12)

Halftime: the Sacrament of Reconciliation. (102-103)

Hits: unexpected negative events that happen to us and trigger a response or reaction. (145)

Holiness: the constant pursuit of our True Purpose. (6)

In the Moment (ITM): immediately addressing sudden and unanticipated challenges that invite us to choose EGO over our True Purpose. (93)

Indicators: person-specific feelings and physical responses that alert us that we are Below the Line. (79)

Inside Job: learning to align one's thoughts, passions, and desires with God's will by actively learning to PATH in the yoke with Jesus. (28)

Invitations: person-specific events and circumstance that influence us to go Below the Line. (79)

IQ (Intelligence Quotient): raw brain power; book smarts. (39)

Justice: genuine concern and desire for each person's right to be respected; working to think and act honorably towards others. (24)

Kingdom of Heaven: the establishment of God's Will on earth; when all creation lives out its purpose and fundamental nature. (9)

Law of 90/10: 90% of our happiness is rooted in what we do on The Inside and only 10% is linked to what is happening Out There. (28)

Law of Big Things: when parent gives Space and teen handles Space responsibly, parent has greater Peace of Mind and gives more Space. (122)

Law of Conviction: the more we believe something to be true, the truer it is for us. (98)

Law of Opposites: the antidote for any temptation or Negative Thinking Habit can be found in a virtue. (91)

L-E-T Method: a three-tier approach for successfully ending a relationship: limit time, expand circle of friends, terminate. (130-131)

Line, The: a metaphor for understanding our state of mind, moods or attitudes as being Above the Line and serving us well or Below the Line and not in our best interest. (76)

LOST (Let Other Stuff Triumph): linking our happiness to factors outside our sphere of influence, such as objects, activities, fame, fortune, status, and other people's opinions. (12)

Mentor: an older, more experienced person whose wisdom can help us keep on the PATH while navigating events and experiences in the Land of Other People. (133)

Monitoring Chit-Chat: a metaphor for bringing self-awareness to the internal dialogue taking place within us; reveals the presence and manipulations of the Evil Emperor. (94-95)

Moral Virtues: any attitude or frame of mind that leads to the PATH by enabling us to opt for doing the holy, God-seeking thing in a given situation. (21)

Mystical Body of Christ, The: the mystery by which the baptized members of the Church become part of Jesus Christ's own body and, therefore, part of each other. (107)

Name It, Claim It, Tame It: a technique for addressing a temptation, Negative Thinking Habit, or problem by clearly identifying it, accepting responsibility for it, and doing something to diminish or remove it. (92)

Negative Thinking Habits (NTHs): person-specific attitudes, beliefs, opinions, or ways of thinking that sabotage our ability to PATH; the weapons of the Evil Emperor. (72)

New Adam, The: title given to Jesus reflecting his mission to live fully and completely the True Purpose of humans by living perfectly our fundamental nature as made in God. (66)

Not Now: a technique used to eliminate distractions or negative thoughts. (88)

Original Holiness: enjoying pure and true happiness by finding one's fundamental purpose united with and living in God. (64)

Parking Lot, The: a metaphor for temporarily storing distractions or negative thoughts. (88)

PATH (Pursue All Things Holy): the fundamental commitment to pursuing all beliefs, choices, and behaviors that are directly aligned with knowing and loving God completely and fiercely and loving other people in God's name. (6)

Peace of Mind (POM): a parent's feeling of well-being when kids are safe and growing in virtue. (121)

Plank: a thought pattern, habit, opinion, or belief that impedes our ability to see a person or situation correctly. (48)

Potential: that which can develop or become actual; possibility. (8)

Prudence: to look at a situation and recognize correctly what is right and wrong, good and evil. (24)

Pure of Heart: having one's heart and mind in sync with the will of God. (154)

Review Your Videos (see also Examen): daily reflection over the events, interactions, and outcomes of our day with particular effort made to recognize God's presence and identify planks and temptations. (100)

Rewriting: a technique used to 'erase' thoughts that are not serving our True Purpose by reshaping them in a more beneficial way. (93-94)

Sacrament of the Present Moment, The: spiritual belief expressed by Pierre de Caussade that every person, interaction, and situation is designed to help us move further along the PATH. (110)

Safeguards of Peace: our role as mediators of good will and harmony resulting from our nature as made in the image of God. (139)

Saint: a role model for the PATH whose excellence in behavior, example, or success deserves to be imitated. (135)

Submarine: a metaphor for maintaining dignity and protecting others and ourselves when we go Below the Line. (80)

Success Formula, The (S = VQ x IQ): academic and career success are a function of our Virtue Quotient (virtues attained) and our Intelligence Quotient (book smarts). (40)

Temperance: control over one's impulses, actions, and passions. (25)

Temptation: a Negative Thinking Habit, choice, behavior, or habit that penetrates the vulnerable spots of the soul and exposes us to the workings of the Evil Emperor. (91)

Thought Circle: powerful negative thinking patterns that develop rapidly and are likely to occur when we are LOST or Below the Line. (84)

Toe-to-Toe: the LOST approach to resolving a conflict; a win-lose method resulting in benefits for one and losses for the other. (152)

Tornado: the invisible, destructive power of negative social interactions. (139)

Trampoline: an activity that assists us in rebounding from Below the Line to Above the Line. (81)

True Happiness: rooted in gratitude to God for the gift of life; realized by pursuing all things holy. (17)

True Purpose: to know and love God completely and fiercely and to love other people in God's name; to be holy and to PATH. (6)

Trust Fund: a savings account metaphor measuring the health and strength of a relationship. (114)

ULC (Upper Left Corner): the beginning of the Framing process; refers to one's thoughts, beliefs, and opinions; the focal point of the intimate relationship between an individual and Jesus. (34)

VQ (Virtue Quotient): the reservoir of inner skills and virtues which sustains an individual's pursuit of all things holy. (39)

Win-Win: the PATH approach to resolving a conflict by seeking benefit for both people. (153)

Withdrawal: a negative act that diminishes a trust fund. (115)

Yoke: the intimate relationship between an individual and Jesus; allows the individual to receive guidance and mercy, avoid temptation, and bear much fruit. (29)

About the Author

Today's Catholic teens stand at the gateway of a life-long expedition. They are looking for relevant content, personal faith, and concrete strategies that help them keep to the Path during turbulent and tempting times.

Peg Dubrowski is a veteran Catholic school teacher who has spent 20+ years inviting teens on this adventure of a lifetime: the quest for personal and profound faith in Jesus Christ. Like so many Catholic educators, she mined the resources available and found herself wishing for more: resources written in a voice teens can relate to, with timely references, age-appropriate spiritual direction, and approaches that foster the mindset, habits, and choices of Jesus.

In 2006, Peg encountered the Top 20 Teens program. Top 20's dynamic metaphors speak to teens, their parents, and their teachers with a freshness and accessibility that would make Jesus, the man of tailor-made parables, proud. With Top 20 founder Paul Bernabei's generosity and critical feedback, Peg conceived, created and directed an active discipleship program for Catholic teens. It harnesses the dynamite metaphors of Top 20 to the beauty, truth and power of our Catholic faith. The resulting synergy is testimony to the vibrant work of the Holy Spirit. *On the PATH* is the student component of this program.

Peg is a charismatic and engaging motivational speaker. She is available for student leadership training, retreats, youth rallies, faculty training days, and parent workshops. She can be contacted at peg@onthepathbooks.com or at her website, onthepathbooks.com.

TOP 20 TRAINING and EDUCATIONAL MATERIALS

Mission: To enable people to discover their potential to make a positive difference in their lives and the lives of others by providing Top 20 training and materials..

Training: Sessions are scheduled to meet the particular needs of a school, group or district. Specific training is available for:

Educators: **Creating a Culture of Learning and Engaging Disengaged Students**
Creating an Effective and Healthy Workplace Culture

Students: **Becoming the Best Version of Yourself** -- Grades 5-12; 2-3 hours; topics include living Above the Line, listening in the zone, helping others succeed, eliminating negativity, celebrating confusion and making things better after messing up.
Dare to Lead: Grades 7-12; 2 hours; topics include being your true self, making and learning from mistakes and challenging negativity.
Removing Negativity from Tween/Teen Girl Culture: Grades 5-12; 1½ hours; topics include eliminating gossip, rumors and 'mean girl' behavior.

Parents: **Guiding Our Children Through Life's Challenges**

Online Training Programs for Teachers and Parents

Training Modules: include detailed facilitator's guide, videos, power point and handouts enabling you to conduct an outstanding Top 20 training in your own school on the following topics.

Top 20 Teachers and Students Live Above the Line
Top 20 Teachers and Students Know How to See Things Differently
Top 20 Teachers and Students Learn from Mistakes
Top 20 Teachers and Students Keep Stupid in the Box
Top 20 Teachers and Students Create a Culture of Safety

Books: *Top 20 Teachers: The Revolution in American Education*
Top 20 Teens: Discovering the Best-kept Thinking, Learning and Communicating Secrets of Successful Teenagers
Top 20 Parents: Raising Happy, Responsible and Emotionally Healthy Children
Following Jesus On the PATH: A Catholic Teen's Guide to Life-Altering Faith
Why Students Disengage in American Schools and What We Can Do About It

Teacher Manuals: Include detailed lesson plans for Top 20 concepts and student handouts
For Grades K-6: *TLC: Thinking, Learning and Communicating*
For Grades 7-12: *Top 20 Teens*

Contact info: www.top20training.com 651-308-4876 info@top20training.com